To Paul -
With Best Wishes
for the Next
"Season" of your
Life.

Andy Fleming

Getting Ahead
Without
Losing Heart

Getting Ahead Without Losing Heart

Andrew T. Fleming

Foreword by
James W. Fowler

Frederic C. Beil
Savannah

Published in the United States of America by
Frederic C. Beil, Publisher, Inc.
609 Whitaker Street
Savannah, Ga. 31401
http://www.beil.com

First edition

LIBRARY OF CONGRESS CATALOGING-IN-PUBLICATION DATA
Fleming, Andrew T. (Andrew Thompson), 1958–
Getting ahead without losing heart / by Andrew T. Fleming;
foreword by James W. Fowler.
p.   cm.
Includes bibliographical references (p.   ).
ISBN 0-913720-64-X (alk. paper)
1. Conduct of life–United States–Case studies.
2. Success–United States–Case studies.
3. Interviews–United States.
4. United States–Biography.
I. Title.
BJ1547.4.F54   1999   99-12843
170 ' .44–dc21   CIP

This book was set in the Galliard typeface by SkidType, Savannah, Georgia;
and printed on acid-free paper.

The poem "Dark Night," from *Backing Down the Ladder* (1998)
by Andrew T. Fleming, is reprinted with permission of
New Visions Press.

To
My Parents
Robert and Oma Lou Fleming

Dark Night

Alone, empty apartment
furniture repossessed
Am I mad?

Voices, voices

*"You can explain one mistake
on your resume but not another."*

*"You're a wild man.
You have no business writing a book now."*

$50,000 in school loans assumed
I would follow the path.
I mortgaged my future
for a ticket I do not want.

Hardest voice of all to hear:
"I did this to myself."

Only in retrospect a turning point.
Only in retrospect I thank God
for dark nights.

—Andrew T. Fleming

Contents

Foreword

THIS BOOK SHOULD WEAR the warning label *DANGER, PROCEED WITH CAUTION, CONTENTS MAY BE HAZARDOUS TO THE PATH YOU ARE ON!* Readers will find the seven stories presented here engaging in their drama, moving in their candor, and stimulating in very deep ways. Andy Fleming's book explores the arenas of love and work, of marketing and meaning, of ambition and service, of success and the search for rewarding ways of living. This is a book about success that includes a full accounting of the need for integrity, for spirit, for friendship, for contributions to the common good, and for joy in the work we do.

Choate, Yale, Harvard Business School, athletic success, prestigious companies—Fleming epitomized the "fast track." On the way, however, he found himself running with half a lung and half a heart. He found the courage and stubbornness to get off the track and begin a process of shaping an alternate path. During the year of making that decision, he interviewed seven men and women who were his peers and friends (or friends of friends). Successful competitors in law, finance, marketing, and technology management, they shared with Andy the paths they had shaped and their present assessments of how they were doing. Each one brings a quality of integrity and honesty you will find moving.

For the past five years Andy Fleming has been director of Leadership and Life-Work in the Center for Ethics of Emory University. In that capacity he has utilized the experiences and insights he gained in this writing, and since, to work with hundreds of Emory students. He has also worked with leaders at all levels in some of this country's top companies. His workshops and courses provide safe space to begin or deepen the clarification of direction and purpose that *Getting Ahead Without Losing Heart* points toward. Last year he published his first book of poetry, a powerful collection of original meter and imagery arising from the journey that began with the stories you will find here and the story he is living.

The book you hold in your hands will hold your attention and your heart. Andy has added reflective guides for each of the stories, should you want to use them as mirrors for self-reflection, and as stimuli for assessing and reshaping your path. He has added a generous list of books and films he has found catalytic for persons and groups who want to work on these themes. The book is a great one for study or discussion groups.

It has been my joy to be part of Andy's life as he has lived with the themes of this book and brought it to completion. Frederick Buechner, novelist and essayist, writes: "The place God calls you to is the place where your deep gladness and the world's deep hunger meet." This book will make that statement intelligible, and provide bread for your journey of calling and gladness.

JAMES W. FOWLER, PH.D.
Director, Center for Ethics, Emory University
January 1999

Preface

I BEGAN WRITING THIS BOOK twelve years ago. I started because I did not like what I was doing and where I was headed just five months after graduating from Harvard Business School. Instead of switching to another lane of the fast track, as others expected and my financial circumstances demanded, I decided to do something different, probably crazy. I set out to write a book that might help others avoid my fate—and that might assure those already in a similar position and frame of mind that they were not alone.

Getting Ahead Without Losing Heart chronicles how I spent the next year, leaving my job with a prestigious company and attempting to write such a book. In addition to my own narrative of "dark nights" and eventful days, this book features seven stories of current and former fast trackers speaking in their own voices about how they have made educational and career choices. I include a Wall Street trader who dreams of becoming a doctor, a Dartmouth graduate who becomes a hotel desk clerk, and a marketing manager who risks her health and family to climb the corporate ladder.

I hope that you will find these stories as entertaining and compelling as I did and that they will serve you, as they did me, as a kind of mirror for looking at your own choices and orientation to life and as a stimulus for attending to the movements of your heart. I offer this book, which includes reflective exercises after each chapter and a listing of other books and films, from my heart to yours.

Acknowledgments

I FEEL PRIVILEGED AND GRATEFUL for the generosity of seven young adults who shared with me their educational and career journeys—and allowed me to offer their stories to others. In order to maintain confidentiality, I have altered their names and the names of the institutions with which they are associated, as well as other nonessential details of their narratives. I do, however, wish to name other special people who helped make this book possible. I am especially indebted to my parents for their love and support always, and to my brother, Scott Fleming, the Reverend Bruce Bunker, Dr. Stephen A. Stumpf, Dr. James W. Fowler, Kathleen Kinlaw, and Claire Lee.

I am also deeply grateful for help and encouragement from Shirley Allen, Jenifer Bidwell, Carl Brown, Stacia Brown, Libby Christian, George Dershimer, Greg Davis, Jonathan Dolger, Harriet Hamilton, Cynthia Joyce, Barbara Klatchko, Carol Mann, Jeff Montie, Maureen Morse, Steve Olson, M. Scott Peck, Donna Price, Steve Rogers, Steven Rothman, Peter Schultz, Heath Smith, Beth Sweetland-Bailey, Linn Ann Tyrrell, Melissa Wiginton, Larry and Nancy Zigerelli, the brothers of Alpha Tau Omega (Emory University chapter), the Future Thinking Community, and my Monday-night and lay ministry groups.

For her design, editorial, and business acumen—as well as her friendship—I thank my agent, Lana Weber, of the Writers Resource Group.

Finally, for the care and attention given to this book by Frederic C. Beil, my publisher, and for the kindness of Mary Ann Bowman Beil, who brought us together, I am enormously grateful.

*Getting Ahead
Without
Losing Heart*

Reality Check

DID I HAVE IT MADE OR WHAT? Five months after graduating from the Harvard Business School and six years after receiving a B.A. from Yale University, I was making a very good salary and headed for more. A bright future? More chief executive officers come from Yale than any other college and from Harvard than any other business school. And Procter & Gamble is renowned as a breeding ground for successful corporate climbers.

In fact, P&G—Pampers, Folgers, Charmin, Tide, Cheer, Ivory, Dawn, etc.—is the king of consumer products marketing. Many other well-run companies have copied their brand management system, their advertising techniques, and, sometimes, even their products. If someone wants to master the consumer products marketing game, he or she can find no better place to learn than Procter & Gamble. But after five months in their prestigious Packaged Soap Division, I was not such a someone. For sixty hours a week I wrangled over things like the color of letters and the wording of "net weight statements" on soap boxes.

"White or red?"

"And should we print the number of ounces or the number of uses? Or both?"

Of course I had other responsibilities, but those were two of the "big" issues I handled. I expended so much time and energy at work for so little satisfaction. Others at P&G would say, "Wait until you get to see your box on store shelves all over the country." Somehow, I did not think that was going to be a big thrill. But I cannot blame P&G for my unhappiness. In a multimillion-dollar product launch, painstaking research and debate should accompany every detail of a marketing program, including the color of letters. Nonetheless, I hated dragging myself out of bed every morning and heading toward the P&G offices, battling with well-entrenched staff groups, trying to slay the bureaucratic dragon.

And I had been warned about this, too. After I had completed one of those standardized, self-assessment tests at Harvard, a career counselor there said: "This test measures how well you would fit in a large, bureaucratic organization, such as the Army or a Fortune 500 company. The higher the score, the better the fit. On a scale of zero to sixty, you scored a minus four."

I should have paid more attention to that counselor. I should have, but I did not. I thought I wanted to be a manager, a position that, in my mind, assumed heroic proportions. As I said in my business school applications, I wanted to "marshal resources" and "attack problems" and "lead other people to worthy goals." Looking back, I think I wanted to become the managerial equivalent of Wyatt Earp—hard-boiled, tough but fair, calculating but also compassionate. I would earn my badge at the Harvard Business School and ride off to help companies protect and enhance their market share. But a few months after arriving, this gunslinger wanted to get the hell out of Dodge City.

Was I a coward? Just not tough enough to face the bureaucratic battles that all would-be managers must survive? And did I really give the company and the job my best effort? Was five months long enough to have taken my best shots?

I did not have the answers to those questions, but I also could not see my attitude improving much in the months to come.

One day in November, after a particularly frustrating meeting, a close friend at work took a look at the battle-weary expression on my face and said, "Why do I have the feeling that this was a significant day in your life?"

Jeff's intuition was right; his timing was just a little off. The big day came later. At the end of November I was just starting to look back and wonder how I had gotten myself into this increasingly agonizing position.

I thought about ten years spent at some of the finest schools in the country—Choate, Yale, and Harvard Business School—and how I still did not know what I wanted out of a career, or out of my life.

I thought about being $50,000 in debt and how that seemed to limit my options. I could not really drop off the fast track, not with loan payments of over $500 a month. But I also thought about how miserable it would be to continue on indefinitely in my current job, or a similar one at another company. Day after day, week after week—Man, this is my life we're talking about here.

In addition to looking at my own situation, I wondered if some of my peers were also questioning their educational and career choices. What had they gone through? How much satisfaction had they found? And how did they feel about their journey now?

I began to feel that asking them about their lives might help me to sort out my own, or at least give me a fresh perspective. And one idea kept flashing through my mind: that a collection of interviews—perhaps even a book—might be helpful to others as well. I decided to try an interview and see what I could learn.

The Writer: Scott Harris

"I don't worry if my present life-style is in sync with my Ivy League background anymore."—Scott Harris

WHEN WE WERE GROWING UP, I thought my best friend, Scott Harris, and I had a lot in common. Both of us were tall and skinny, very athletic, good students, and shy around girls. And we both went to Choate/Rosemary Hall and then to Ivy League colleges. A year older, I used to think he was following in my footsteps. I do not think that way anymore.

Scott taught fifth- and sixth-grade English at a private school for two years after graduating from Dartmouth. Then he quit his job and began working at a motel as a part-time desk clerk in the evenings, living off his $5.00/hour salary and occasional stints as a substitute teacher. In his spare time Scott now works on the short novel he has been writing for the past year. He pays $175/month for a studio apartment in a blue-collar Midwestern town of forty thousand, and his significant possessions include Salvation Army–type furniture, a fifteen-year-old car, and a ten-year-old stereo. The man does not even own a TV.

Funny thing, from all I could tell, Scott was a lot happier than I. So, over one weekend, I drove from Cincinnati to Mishawaka, Indiana, to ask him how he felt about the path he has taken.

I went to Choate because it was the established pattern in my family. My two older brothers had gone there, so I didn't really think about going to the public high school. It seemed as if this was what the family was doing. Then, when you're twelve years old, you don't put a lot of thought into anything like that. It wasn't a conscious decision. It just seemed like the thing to do.

At the time I didn't know what I was getting into. I didn't know it would be a real different life at one place as opposed to the other. I suppose I sensed to a degree.

Choate cuts you off from your hometown and the simple things that one associates with high school. They weren't a part of Choate. We were in an environment of people who were coming from different parts of the country, who had very different backgrounds. We were kind of thrown into that mishmash, and, socially, we lost touch with many of our public school friends.

It seemed as if the people who came to Choate from outside Wallingford had more sophistication than the townspeople did. That may have been an illusion, but it seemed they were more worldly than I was, certainly. But then again, I look at myself as a pretty naive kid, too, so my own nature may have come into play with that as opposed to anything that was inherent in those people or inherent in the school itself.

Anyway, that was my perception, and it just made me not hang out with most Choaties. I'd hang out with those other people who shared the same situation with me—the local townspeople who went to Choate. I was a lot more comfortable with them. And so, in a way, I was not only a foreigner to many of my old public school friends, but also to those more "worldly" people who were coming into Choate.

On top of that, Choate was a very demanding school, and I've always been *outrageously* conscientious. I think there's an imbalance in my head where I can't not do the work that's assigned to me—even when I hate it and find it inherently meaningless. I can't *not* do it, you know . . . I certainly didn't work as hard as I did because of a real interest in the material or a great desire to learn the stuff. And, truthfully, I don't think I was motivated that much by a desire to get good grades—though, of course, as a prep school student it's always drummed into you how important it is to get good grades and to have a good record so you can go to a good college. Definitely I was no exception—I thought about that stuff, too. But I think that the main reason I worked as hard as I did was not for some big future goal, like going to college; I think it was more out of fear over my performance in the next day's classes. I always had a fear of getting caught with my pants down, that's all. You don't want to go through that—getting called on and not having your homework done and not being able to offer a good explanation. And I'm a terrible "BSer"—I can't make things up on the spot to make it seem like I know what I'm talking about. So if I didn't do my homework, I was really lost.

With me, though, sometimes it didn't even matter that I'd done my homework thoroughly—I could get humiliated in class anyway. I wasn't too heavy into class discussion; I was basically a quiet guy. And maybe I'd be in a class where we were discussing the symbolism in a Nathaniel Hawthorne short story, or maybe in a history class we'd be discussing the significance or the soundness of some big decision by a political leader; and everybody would be talking, throwing in their two cents worth, and I'd be sitting there listening to it all, wondering how people could have real live opinions about all this stuff. And me, I didn't care about it or have one little thing to say about it at all. But then at some point the teacher would disrupt the conversation and turn to me and say, "Scott, we haven't heard from you yet. What's your opinion of such-and-such?" And I'd go, "Well . . . " And everybody's face would turn toward me, and I'd be aware of my face turning red; then I'd start making sounds: "Ummm, well, blah, glaa, bluh . . ." Then to save face I'd agree with what someone else said—"I think that, ah, what so-and-so-said . . . " Or if it was an English class you could always say that whatever was being discussed seemed to serve as a Christ symbol. That would usually bring a hush over the crowd.

Whenever I'd have a private conference with teachers, they'd always encourage me to talk more in class. They'd say, "Now I know there are interesting things going on in your head, Scott, because you write such thoughtful papers." And I'd sit there and nod and maybe mumble a promise that I'd try to contribute more in the future, but inside I was screaming at them—No, you've got it all wrong! There's really nothing going on inside my head when you call on me. Absolutely nothing! I may look like I'm pondering something, but you're misreading me. I don't have opinions about any of this stuff.

So my number one goal in working as hard as I did was to minimize the amount of attention drawn to me in class, and the best way to do that was by being fully prepared. And at Choate, if you did everything that was assigned to you, and you were not a quick worker, which I wasn't, then you worked your butt off. Almost every evening was spent working. It could go up to five or six hours per night for a really intense period. And it rarely went below two or three. It was definitely a good chunk of the evening.

The only possible free time I had was in the afternoon, but athletics were required then. And I'd have to say that playing basketball didn't add a lot to my Choate experience. In fact, now that I think about it, I hated basketball with a passion. I hated it probably more than working. At least at times. I hated being winded; I hated doing drills; and I didn't particularly like the coaches or the other players, either. Other than that, it was a real kick.

Baseball was a different story, though. For one thing, you didn't have to run as much, which was great with me. But also I had a degree of success in baseball, too, which was nice. On the junior varsity and the varsity, I wasn't too bad, I think. I surprised a lot of people with that—surprised myself. Definitely, pitching was a kick. I particularly liked that there's a lot of outguessing involved— outguessing the batter—and I remembered how I liked that you're "the man" out there. All eyes are focused on you, and you dictate the pace of the game; nothing happens until you put the ball in play. Actually, I guess you could say it was kind of a bizarre role for a guy who was so reserved and passive to be all of a sudden the center in front of everybody, and be "the man" out there. It's true that the team behind you has to make the plays, but you've got to pitch the batters right. You've got to make them hit the ground ball or strike them out. And when you're successful, you're just like king of the world, and so that was kind of a rush for me.

Pitching is also a way of being noticed, particularly if you're doing well. You're standing out there, and all eyes are on you without you having to assert yourself directly to another person. Pitching made me feel like some girls might notice me. There were times when I'd pick her out. I'd check out the crowd, see who was there, and dedicate a pitch to this brunette. I hoped that someone might fall in love with me by the way I threw a curveball. But it never did happen. You know, you've got to talk to girls too. You can't just pitch in front of them all the time.

So with all of my time divided up between classes, athletics in the afternoon, and homework at night, I really didn't have much time for anything else. If I'd gone to a public school instead of Choate, I don't know if I'd have immersed myself in more activities and social things that would have done a lot of good for me or whether I just would've wasted time or horsed around, just been a kid. I would've felt more comfortable at a public school, I think. And I wouldn't have been in awe of the people and the environment around me. But whether I'd have gotten involved in different types of organizations or stuff like that, I don't know . . . I really don't.

I think back to my own nature, particularly back then, which was not very aggressive or outgoing. I'd never be the one to really take the initiative in a lot of things. I just did what I was supposed to do at Choate. And I can't look back and say there was something else that I really wanted to do instead—something that I really had a burning desire to do. I don't know of anything I really had a burning desire to do as a thirteen or fourteen-year-old kid. There are a lot of little things that maybe I would've done, which would've been a kick had I not been in this environment—just horsing around more would have been one. But I was so swamped in this work.

Looking back now, though, I don't feel I have any real regrets about my past at Choate, just because now I feel I'm where I want to be, and I'm doing what I want to do. And if you tamper with anything in the past, who knows how you would be changed now. *Now* seems pretty cool, so I don't look back on things with regrets—even though sometimes I think I probably would've fit in better and had some happier times if I'd gone to public school.

And if I hadn't gone to Choate, particularly with having older brothers there, my view of Choate as an outsider might have made me feel not so good about being in a public school. I might have always looked at Choate as a "better" world, as a place where you get more educated and where your opportunities in life are greater for having gone there. And I might have thought myself a schmo, you know, because I didn't get out of me as much as I could have gotten out of me.

Was it valuable to have been pushed as hard as you were in academics?

Probably not. I think it's hard to say, but probably not. If I were to look back at that isolated time period right then, and just look at that individual, I would probably say it would have been best for that individual to have grown in other areas besides just working his tail off.

I do think it's good to prove to yourself that you can work hard. But I could have proved that at the start in a week or so; it didn't have to be four years.

After Choate I wasn't really focused on what I would do next, although college was certainly a given. In our family there was no discussion about whether or not you were going to college; it was just accepted that you were going, which was fine with me.

When I went up to visit Gene (my older brother) at Dartmouth, the fraternity atmosphere there really opened up my eyes. I saw a lot of people there who seemed to be having a good time. And, God knows, I was ready for some of that. I'm sure that it was all a reaction to the one-dimensional life of academics that I had at Choate. Here was another dimension that would hopefully help me with the social world, which Choate didn't seem to do at all. I was very taken by the carefree revelry of the fraternities.

I also knew Dartmouth means a lot of prestige, and I can't say I ignored that aspect. Just as I knew Choate was more prestigious than most public schools, I knew Dartmouth was more prestigious than a number of other colleges that I could have gone to. So I got the two things I wanted: the prestige of going to a really respected school and the chance to get involved in something other than academic life. In fact, when I was a college freshman, I remember trying to be a real part of the "Dartmouth world." I tried to be a

9

real Dartmouth party animal. Rah, rah, school spirit—all that stuff that is easy for a freshman to get swept up in. My whole first year I concentrated on that.

Pretty soon, though, I started to become disillusioned with the whole atmosphere. I wasn't feeling like a real part of the fraternity world—where everybody seemed to be having a good time—and I didn't feel that what I had hoped for was working out. There were some sad times when I'd get real bummed out. I felt out on the fringe, you know.

It's funny how when you first go into a different environment— a new school, a new town—you think things are really going to change in your life, that you'll be a different person there. Then six months later you realize that you've established yourself, for the most part, in the same way you were in your previous environment. As it turns out, of course, it doesn't matter where you are physically; it matters what you're like inside. When I went to Dartmouth, I was excited about the possibility of a "new me," but I was really the same guy. Only time can change you, I guess, not simply placing yourself in a different environment.

Ultimately what I did throughout the rest of my time at Dartmouth was balanced between being on the fringe of the party world and removing myself from it completely. On weekends a friend of mine and I would just leave campus completely and check out the bars and rock clubs in the small neighboring towns. That was my way of escaping. The fraternity brothers weren't too crazy about me taking off on weekends to go to these bars; they wanted you to hang around and go to all the house functions. But a lot of the time I just had to get away.

On the academic side, I wasn't really focused either going into my sophomore year. I became an English major, primarily by default at first. I'd tried a number of different subject areas as a freshman; I'd taken a couple of economics courses, some history, philosophy— none of them really did that much for me. In my English classes, though—although I really didn't get into a lot of the stuff that we were reading—at least I felt that interesting things were being said in class a lot of the time. And there were some writers that I did feel kind of drawn toward, like Whitman, whom now I really love, and

Thoreau; and Emerson I thought was great. All of these nineteenth-century romantics, I guess. And then I took a class with one of the "radical" professors on campus, and he taught writers who are pretty much the twentieth-century descendants of Whitman and Thoreau. It was in his class that I began reading writers like Henry Miller, Thomas Wolfe, and Jack Kerouac. These guys spoke in a more contemporary voice, so it was easier for me to relate to it and be affected by it. And I just basically ate the stuff up.

Here was something I genuinely started to believe in—and for a while there I felt I was exploding inside. Their writing was really lyrical, and their outlook—I guess you could call it pantheistic, though some people might not agree with that, particularly with a writer like Miller. Some people probably consider their writing just really "antiestablishment" and anti-everything, but what I got from them was a sense of affirmation more than anything else—affirmation that it's a wonderful thing to be a human being and that there are a lot of good things in life—intangible things. Another important part of their writing was relentless self-examination, and I was really drawn to this aspect of their work, too. Ultimately, they made me reexamine my values and the values of the people around me at college. And I started to change.

I became passionate about these writers and a number of others like them. I felt I had something I actually believed in—not something I accepted because it was the norm around me. But at the same time that I became excited about this stuff it became harder for me to exist at a conservative school like Dartmouth. I'd turned into a naive romantic—something that I think a lot of college students turn into when they're first profoundly affected by something they've read. It's not that I really changed much on the outside; I was still my same old quiet self when it came to the academic world and the social world, etc. I was just different on the inside. But of course I struggled with the values of getting good grades, and of getting a good job after college—you don't just erase values that have been a part of your life for six or seven years. In addition, I felt that I owed my parents quite a bit, too. They'd made sacrifices to put me through college—and I wouldn't have felt right if after finishing, I didn't do what was expected of any Ivy

League graduate, which is, of course, to go out and get a decent, respectable job. I can't say that they put any pressure on me to do this, but I knew that this is what you do after you graduate from Dartmouth.

So I started thinking about a job that would be in sync with my training and in sync with the prestige of the school. I can remember once—I've always been passionate about music and I worked at the Dartmouth radio station for a while—briefly thinking that I wouldn't mind being a disc jockey for some sort of alternative rock station or something like that. But I bagged the idea real quickly because it didn't seem like you could go to Dartmouth in order to spin records in a studio after graduation. Eventually I became really bored with working at the radio station anyway, so it's not as if I ended up stifling any great ambition.

When I was thinking about a job for after graduation, the notion that it had to be a "respectable" one was definitely in my head. I eventually decided to give teaching a try. But I have to admit that I was never really motivated to be a teacher, never driven. I just thought it would be okay because I knew I could deal with the subject matter, English, and because society puts a stamp of approval on someone who decides to become a teacher. It's viewed as kind of a noble thing to build future minds and all that. And also, I really liked kids. Maybe my ideas about them have changed a bit after having worked with them in the classroom for a couple of years. But back then I especially liked kids around the ages of eleven and twelve.

So I ended up spending the two years after graduation as a sixth-grade English teacher at a private school in Indiana. The first year went okay. I wasn't passionate about it or anything, but it was going well enough that I decided to stay for another year. But it was early in the second year that I realized there were things about teaching that I simply was not going to be able to deal with any more. It seemed like a counterproductive, almost evil thing to do, to hold out an "A" like it was some kind of candy. I guess I've never been really fond of the system of giving out grades. And I liked it even less when I was on the other end—the one giving them out. Especially to little kids, you know. God, I really do think it's a screwed up thing to do. But I also didn't like the amount of time I had to spend on things like correcting papers and coaching. Actually, I can't say I disliked coaching; it's just that all of these time-consuming things meant that I had to deny the part of myself that was passionately interested in literature and writing.

I did care about the kids, no question about that, and I hoped that I was doing them some good; but my growing dissatisfaction with teaching became a kind of desperation. Finally, I was sitting with the gym teacher from the school at McDonald's after a fifth- and sixth-grade softball game, and we were talking about our futures—we had both started the same year—and I told her that if I didn't quit after this year, I was going to drive my car off a cliff or something. So she and I decided that, yeah, it was probably time for me to go.

When I left teaching, my intention was simply to write. Ever since I was a junior in college, I'd done some writing off and on, sporadically. Back then all of it was spurred on by the writers that I was really excited about—and all of it was very imitative of these writers. And now I really can't even bring myself to read any of my writing from back then. But while I was teaching, I always still had writing in the back of my mind, and as time went on, I felt myself more and more driven to give it a serious shot.

I guess I've grown to believe that you have to respond to your strong interests, your passions, no matter where they might lead you. You have to live them out. Otherwise, you live a lie your whole life. Sometimes I used to think what it would be like to be seventy-five or eighty years old and you're sitting in a nursing home or wherever, and you're pretty much living through your memories. I don't think you'd care much about the things you'd achieved if throughout your whole life you'd denied that which was inherently important to you. That's the real horror for me— a life full of activity, but in which you wake up some morning and realize that you've done all these things, but when it comes right down to it, you haven't pursued your true inclinations. And on top of that you really don't know anything about yourself. You'd feel like you'd never lived, period. God, that would suck.

So, anyway, when I finally did quit teaching I had no set plans in my head, but the writing side of me had been pent up for so long that I really didn't have a choice except to deal with it. And I was convinced that I would be writing something very soon.

Then, the first year or so I'd come up with some ideas for a short story or a longer work and I'd try to work them out; but after a week or so they'd fall apart. And I'd start to wonder. The walls would kind of cave in on me and I'd think: What the hell are you doing with yourself? You're no good at this. And you're running out of money. What are you doing with your *life*?

So, yeah [laughs] there were times then when I was kind of freaking out—when I was first unemployed and was trying to become a writer and was getting nowhere. I felt tremendous pressure. I'd given up on the notion of getting a respectable job and following a path consistent with my background—but you don't just walk away from the things that you once considered important or the values that have been a part of your life over a long period. It takes time to adjust. Your old ways of thinking stay in your mind; you can't just will them to go away because that's what you really want.

What made it even more difficult was that I really wasn't ready to write. I was ready in the sense that I wanted to write; that was my desire. But I wasn't ready in terms of having something to say or a voice through which I could speak. I was just a youngster. And I still am, of course.

When I quit teaching, though, it was a funny period for me, I have to admit. I'd come up with these little reasons why my writing kept failing. I'd say to myself, Okay, you can't be a writer yet because you haven't read enough. All the great writers were voracious readers at one time or another. So for a month I'd read nine or ten hours a day. It was such an unnatural way to live, you know? I'm sure I got some value out of it, but I started going out of my mind after a while—being cooped up in my apartment all the time. So I'd give up on that and try to write for another month and that would fail again. Then I'd tell myself, You can't write yet because you haven't lived enough experiences. So I'd behave like a raving maniac for a month and a half, drinking and going out to bars, acting very irresponsibly in a self-conscious sort of way—

which was also an unnatural way for me to live. That was just taking it to the other extreme. And I'd wake up one day and say, "What are you doing with yourself now? You're becoming some kind of nut." So I'd pull myself together, try writing again, fail, and then come up with another reason why I couldn't write, another reason that would help me cope for a while.

However, as time went on I actually was "living" in my own screwed-up way, and I actually was becoming myself—whatever that means—in my own screwed up way. I think that time had to pass, that's all, time had to pass. And now, in the past year, I've finally written a thing or two that I like, and I can at least see progress in myself as a writer. I don't feel I've come up with anything great, and I haven't finished anything that I'd be ready to try to get published or even show to the world. But I feel that I can see progress that I've made, that I'm getting somewhere.

And as time has passed, I've come to realize that writing is the only thing I *can* do. That's not to say that I don't have talent for other things. I mean I have the ability to do other things. But I've kind of given in to the fact that writing is what I *want* to do. And I've got to do it, that's all.

Now when I have my moments of freaking out, it's not about what I'm doing with my life—I don't worry about whether my present lifestyle is in sync with my Ivy League background anymore; instead, what I worry about is—Am I going to become an okay writer? Am I going to be able to find a voice through which I can speak?

I honestly don't know what path will lead me to that voice, but I have blind faith that in my own screwed-up way I'll find it . . . and that right now maybe I'm even on that path.

Now that I think about it, there still are brief moments when I'll hear about someone I know from Dartmouth who is making zillions of dollars and I'll think, Wow, that guy must really have his act together and he's been really successful. And what have I got for myself? For a moment there I'll be in desperation land; but then a couple of minutes later I'll laugh at myself for having readopted values that aren't mine and that really don't exist for me any more—except in those kinds of brief moments. And those kinds of moments don't come very often any more. As for those people who are out there pursuing high-powered careers and making lots of money, I genuinely hope they're doing well and are happy. That lifestyle isn't for me, that's all.

All I really want to do is make enough money to maintain a cheap little apartment like the one I have here—I love this place— and have enough money to buy books and records that interest me. I don't care about having a TV or a VCR; and I don't care about having a new car. When the old bomb that I have finally breaks down, I'll just substitute-teach during the days until I have enough money to buy another old bomb. And if my stereo ever breaks down, I'll work enough to get that fixed too.

I realize that if I weren't living as I do now, if I weren't pursuing my writing, I'd constantly have to rationalize whatever else it was that I was doing. Because there's nothing else that I *honestly* want to do—except live this way.

Scott's experience and insights gave me another way of looking at my past choices and future opportunities. How many of my choices had been dictated by what I perceived as other's expectations? What might it be like to break from that pattern? And how might I feel about driving a "bomb" like Scott's? These were the questions that stayed with me after talking with Scott in late November.

Then as I began to edit a transcript of our conversation, something else emerged: a kind of inner satisfaction that I could not quite identify. Putting a three-hour interview into a coherent story demanded so much of my energy, concentration, and imagination— so much of me. Late at night, as I sat alone in front of my computer, I felt somehow more fully alive. No bosses. No bureaucracy. The freedom was so exhilarating:

"Hmm . . . that sentence doesn't fit—"

"That paragraph seems awkward—"

"Let's see . . . maybe this'll work . . . Yeah, yeah . . . "

When I finished Scott's story, I knew it was not Pulitzer prize material, but I felt a degree of fulfillment that far exceeded anything I had experienced at P&G. So now all of my rationalizations for staying with the company were set against some increasingly powerful emotions. It would turn out to be no contest.

QUESTIONS, QUOTATIONS, AND EXERCISES

GENERAL:

a. What incidents, images, ideas, or words from this chapter stand out for you?

b. When were you happy, sad, or mad as you read it?

c. What advice would you like to have given Scott?

d. What are the lessons for your life?

FOCUSED:

"I think that the main reason I worked as hard as I did was not for some big future goal, like going to college; I think it was more out of fear over my performance in the next day's classes. I always had a fear of getting caught with my pants down, that's all."

a. Think about three different situations when you have worked really hard. What truly motivates you? What role does fear play? Others' expectations?

b. Under what conditions are you particularly self-motivated? How can you bring about those conditions more often?

c. What de-motivates you? What can you do to deal with those situations?

"Looking back now, though, I don't feel I have any real regrets about my past . . . just because now I feel I'm where I want to be, and I'm doing what I want to do. And if you tamper with anything in the past, who knows how you would be changed now. *Now* seems pretty cool."

a. To what extent are you now "where you want to be" and "doing what you want to do"? Explain.

b. On a scale of one to ten, how "cool" is now for you? Name the three biggest factors affecting your coolness rating.

c. What regrets are you carrying from the past? What will you do with them now?

17

"Sometimes I used to think what it would be like to seventy-five or eighty years old and you're sitting in a nursing home or wherever, and you're pretty much living through your memories. I don't think you'd care much about the things you'd achieved if throughout your whole life you'd denied that which was inherently important to you. That's the real horror for me—a life full of activity, but in which you wake up some morning and realize that you've done all these things, but when it comes right down to it, you haven't pursued your true inclinations. And on top of that you really don't know anything about yourself. You'd feel like you'd never lived, period. God, that would suck."

a. Identify three memories you would like to have when you are seventy-five or eighty.
b. What is the "real horror" for you?
c. What would you like to find about yourself before you die?

The Soap Box

M Y WHEELS WERE SLIPPING off the track at Procter & Gamble. I wanted to work on my book idea—not soap boxes. I spent fewer hours at the office, left details uncovered, and let projects fall behind. More and more I felt I was living a lie at P&G.

Despite my worsening attitude, however, I was told that I would receive an excellent six-month performance review. But that just added to the anguish I felt; it haunted me to hear any praise or encouragement in the midst of my charade.

I tried to project my usual "game face" at work, but there were a few who sensed something amiss. My boss's boss was one. He called me into his office one day and said, "You're smiling, but you don't look happy. Do you want to talk about it?" I did and I didn't.

Even though I liked and trusted this manager, I still struggled to maintain the image of a fast tracker—happy to be there and rarin' to go. What could I say? Certainly not—"I don't like my job, and I don't see how that can possibly change; what I would really like to do is write a book, but I don't have any money." No, this was not the time for the truth, I decided. Even so, on a morning in mid-December, my facade began to crumble.

My ongoing responsibility as a brand assistant was coordinating the design and manufacture of the packaging for a new detergent. And, I was told, I had to do it in record time. Fair enough, I thought. I'll show them what I can do. So I responded to this opportunity by pushing the art department to accelerate their design work on my package. Through repeated phone calls and visits, I personally checked on their progress several times a day. But I did not quite realize what a terror I had become until I was in a department store on a Saturday night. From several aisles away, I heard a familiar voice moan: "I told you that you'll have the drawings first thing Monday morning. Will you please stop following me around?"

I looked over and saw the art director for my project. He was smiling, but he didn't look too happy either. I could not worry much about making him happy, though. Our schedule was too tight for that sort of consideration. And, as I saw it, my job was to give headaches, not get them.

Finally, when I got my hands on a prototype package, I still had to guide it through the P&G artwork approval process. And that is no Sunday drive, even on normal timing. The road toward "final approval" is littered with red tape and the wreckage of many young marketing careers. But I was determined to race my soap box to the finish line on time. I cut a few corners and steered around several staffers who stood in my path. I even convinced one of the regulatory lawyers to give me a green light—on a *Saturday*. That was some kind of fancy driving, I was told.

As time went on, however, I started to get a few headaches of my own. I began to suspect that our project team was caught in one of those "hurry up and wait" situations. As we rushed to ready our product for launch, we were making a lot of lives miserable, including our own, and it seemed likely that our roll-out would get delayed or scrubbed because of a change in soap-market conditions.

So was there really a point to all of our frantic efforts? And just how important was it to provide the world with another laundry detergent, anyway? Even if it was a little easier to use? Or came in an attractive box?

Asking myself those questions began to slow me down. And I almost came to a dead stop when I was told that an upper-level manager wanted to add another word to the name of our product . . . after thousands of boxes were already printed. That meant new artwork, new approvals, and more heat from the rest of the team, no matter how quickly I produced a new box.

I was stunned by the abrupt and, in my mind, unnecessary change. But there was nothing I could do except try to channel some of my anger into energy. And I did, maybe too well. At every step of the redesign process, I was driven by a kind of fast-track machismo. "So that's how they play the game; I'll show 'em who's a real player." Even faster than before, I got my package ready to manufacture.

Well, almost ready. Now every department that had questions about the old design wanted to make last minute changes in the new one. And each little change required new artwork . . . and new artwork required legal approval . . . and lawyers do not like to be rushed. Particularly by a lowly brand assistant for the second time within a month.

But every day I waited for approval meant a one-day delay in the projected launch of our product. And our team did not like talking about delays with upper management. Pressure built. Fingers pointed. Most of them at me.

Finally, after another desperate call to the legal department—a futile effort to get approval for a new "net weight statement"—I snapped. Before hanging up the phone, I felt such rage that I twisted the receiver in my hands and nearly split it in half. Ignoring a noon lunch date, I stormed out of the office on the verge of saying, "That's it! I *quit*. I can't do this anymore!"

Then as I walked toward a nearby Wendy's, I could feel my body beginning to react. My leg muscles started cramping; my hands started shaking. My whole system was in revolt. Inside the restaurant I just sat for a while and stared out the window as the corporate lunch crowd breezed past.

Twelve forty-five. Still on edge. I tried going for a walk; maybe exercise would help. But my legs kept cramping.

"C'mon," I told myself, "you're just doing this so you won't have to go back in there. It's like acting sick to stay home from school."

One-fifteen. Had to get back. I had no idea what I would do, but my mind raced faster and faster the closer I came to the P&G building. Before I reached it, however, I stopped in front of an old church and decided to sit inside. I was not looking for divine guidance. I simply wanted to go, if only for a few moments, where it would be quiet—where nothing was really expected of me—and where, somehow, it would be okay to drop all of the pretenses of the workplace and just be "me."

I stretched out in a back pew and took a few deep breaths. No relief. I kept thinking about my father and the fact that he had spent thirty years with one company. There were times, I knew, when he had "toughed it out." Was that what I should be doing? What was I doing?

Something new flashed into my mind—a poster I'd once seen on a bulletin board, something about a P&G counseling service. Maybe I needed that kind of help.

Half an hour later, I walked back to the office to make a counseling appointment. I struggled to make that call. A real fast tracker keeps his emotions to himself. You want to be known as one of the "can do" types. The "No problem, I'll take care of it" types.

When I spoke to the counselor, I actually had to force the words from my throat. My voice hissed like steam escaping from a radiator, a sound that lasted through meetings with a counselor that night and with my managers the next morning. A sound that prompted the counselor to ask, "Have you had any thoughts of harming yourself?"

No, thankfully I hadn't.

"Well," he said reassuringly, "You're not the first person to have such strong feelings about your job that you want to walk out the door."

Yeah, I knew I was not alone. I had recently conducted my second interview, this time with a former basketball opponent, Terry Ryan. Beyond the fact that we both went to prep school and captained an Ivy League basketball team, Terry and I have another experience in common: we have both derailed along the fast track.

The Stockbroker:
Terry Ryan

"I'd have to say I'm not a very calculating person.
In fact, I'm *frighteningly* uncalculating, to the point
where I'll probably risk taking some wrong
forks in the road."—Terry Ryan

*TERRY RYAN IS THE YOUNGEST of six children from a
middle-class family. Tall and lean, with thick black hair and a
ready smile, Terry immediately comes across as both energetic and
trusting.*

*I had last seen Terry on the basketball court when he played for
Princeton and I was finishing my final season at Yale. Until we met
again seven years later at the home of a mutual friend, all I knew
about Terry was that he could really shoot a basketball.*

*Three hours after we started talking, however, I felt as if Terry and
I were old friends. His experiences came rushing out in great detail,
filled with warmth and good humor. First he related the last-minute
acceptances and mixed feelings that marked his years at two of this
country's most prestigious schools. Then he described his first "real
world" job as a stock trader at a major brokerage firm—an experience that left him searching for answers about the business world,
and, ultimately, about himself.*

I was pretty scared about college because my family had some bad
experiences with it. My one brother had given up on it, going into
the Marines; I had a sister three years older who dropped out after

23

a semester; and I had another older brother who had been a disciplinary problem for my parents—he was a real wild guy. He had gone away to school and then just blown off his second semester to go to Mardi Gras. He just flunked out. It was very intimidating to hear these legendary stories about people in my family having problems in college years—very intimidating. I remember thinking, "Why should I think it's going to be any different for me?" I had this feeling that I might step on a land mine out there, and I didn't want to think about it.

I look back on it, and it's almost spooky. I remember going into my senior year of high school, and I had no idea where I was going to apply to college. No idea. I did have prep school brought up to me my junior year by a few people. This older fellow who was close to me was a big advocate of that. He said, "I've seen a lot of people; you're developing late—you're too young for your grade. You ought to go to the right school and play a good basketball schedule; academically, it's never going to hurt you."

I guess it was in the fall that I realized I had to make some type of decision. I knew that I wanted to play basketball in college. Even though I hadn't been heavily recruited after my junior year, I figured if I had a good senior year things might start to unfold. But the fact of the matter is—if you're a really good player and you're going to play in college, they're going to look at you early in your senior year. By November I wasn't getting hit by a lot of colleges; not many people were interested. One guy I knew from basketball camp did tell me that Dartmouth would be interested in me after prep school. So prep school began to sound like a better idea.

It turned out that a kid from my high school, who had gone to Hotchkiss the year before, was home at Christmas time. He really liked it, and it was obviously considered one of the better places—that much I had heard. But I didn't know anything about prep school other than that. So I set up an appointment to go up there to see the school and see what it was like.

After my interview up there in January, I could have applied to other colleges or prep schools. But I came away from the interview feeling, "Yeah, I think I'd like to go there." I had a good interview;

I had a decent chance of getting in; they were encouraging me; and I just felt it was a warm place. So I didn't apply anywhere else. That was it.

In retrospect, I know it was a decision of major importance, and I can honestly say that there was very little calculation in it. I'd have to say I'm not a very calculating person. In fact, I'm *frighteningly* uncalculating, to the point where I'll probably risk taking some wrong forks in the road.

But I know the process of college and job applications. It's very serious—a very narrow and calculating process. But I've almost felt rebellious about it. I don't respect it because I think it's arbitrary. When you feed yourself into it, you lose your individuality, and I think sometimes it makes grave mistakes with people because of numbers and interviews and things that I don't think are real. So I just didn't get excited about it.

But I did see other kids in my high school fall to their knees because they didn't get into a certain school, and their parents were disappointed, and everybody was disappointed. Well, hell, I'd already seen all that. Everybody before me in my family had gone through that, and you know what? Your life goes on. My brother went into the Marines. My sister dropped out. It's not always happy endings, but you get up the next morning, and you lace up your sneakers, and you do what you've go to do. If you're a father, you make your living. If you're a Marine, you go fight or whatever you do. And so to me, this horror of not getting into XYZ school wasn't that big of a horror because I saw people who didn't get into any school; and they were still my brothers and sisters.

One thing I left out—I did very poorly on my SAT's the first time, absolutely horrible. I got sub-500's on them, and I remember thinking to myself, even though I'd done pretty well in school in areas where I applied myself, "Maybe I am kind of stupid after all, and this test is telling me that." I went through a period of a couple weeks where I really felt down. And then I just decided that these tests aren't that important—they can't be. I have a lot more to offer as a person, and I'm not going to let that test bother me; it's just measuring things wrong. Later I took a coaching course and I did a little better—I got my SAT's up where they were college level in terms of getting into a decent school, but they certainly weren't Ivy League level.

I saw everybody else go through that whole thing with the SAT's; the whole system was crazy. I'd met so many kids from the ghetto by playing basketball outside my hometown, where everybody was fretting about their SAT's. I saw these other kids. Man, they had limited hope . . . very limited. And they were great guys. They were some of the warmest people I'd ever met—very open, very nice, and I became friendly with them about as quickly as I could with anybody else. And, you know, a lot of these things like SAT's weren't problems in their mind.

When I did get accepted to Hotchkiss, a funny thing happened with my high school guidance counselors, who spent more time psychologically helping people with their problems than seeing what you wanted to do about college. They didn't even stay in touch with me and my case. In fact, I remember at the end of my senior year, they came up to me and said, "We're sorry you're not going to college. That's too bad." I said, "Well, I'm not—I'm going to prep school." They didn't even know I had applied. They had just looked at the list of the kids who had gotten into colleges, and I wasn't on it. When I told them I was going to prep school, they said, "That's great—glad we got together on that one."

Prep school turned out to be a fabulous experience in every sense of the word. Going there I had some of those preconceptions: I thought it would be a preppie place, a Waspy place, a place where very wealthy people go and they just take care of their own. But it's like anything else: you find out by meeting the people and seeing the place. You might as well throw out your preconceptions. There's probably good people everywhere, and that's exactly what I found there. On the faculty I met some of the greatest people I've known in academics. They were much more committed to knowing and helping kids than the people from my high school.

I had a history teacher who was the whole reason history became my favorite subject. He had graduated number one from Hotchkiss and number one from Harvard, and then he had gone to Berkeley to get his doctorate. I used to have this negative image of people who were intensely academic—that they were cold and distant. But he was just a very warm, caring, and thoughtful guy who was absolutely brilliant. I had never known anybody like that; he just had a very big influence on me.

The college counselor was also different. He was a hands-on, interested person, a real feisty kind of guy. Two weeks into school, he called me into his office and asked, "Where are you thinking of applying? I've got some names here." I had put the schools that I considered realistically first and then I put some Ivy League schools last. He said, "What are they doing here last?" And I said, "I guess I'll apply." He said, "What do you mean you *guess* you'll apply. You're *going* to apply." He pushed me as if I definitely had a shot to get into a top school, and that was the first time I realized that maybe I did; a lot of it would just depend on my academic record there. But I did have my potential Dunkirk on the academic side, in math. On a scale of zero to six—zero being a failure and six being the best you could do—I got fours in everything but math, where I got a two the first semester. This was just a recurrence of my old record in math. But I knew the second semester was going to be harder, and it was pretty tough for a postgraduate student to fail something and still get into college.

At the same time as I was aware of the math problem, we were having the best basketball season in the school's history. I was with five of the best guys I'd ever played with in terms of being people and players. I had gone from a mediocre small school to a larger school with great players, and we won almost every game. We went to the New England championships and did really well, but the backdrop for me was always, It's not going to mean anything if I don't do well in school. And I knew I was failing math in my second semester.

It was a calculus course that I wasn't up for, and I knew going into the final that it was going to be real tough. And I failed it . . . I failed the course. I remember the triumphant basketball season ending, and I wasn't all that aglow about it; on another front that was part of being at Hotchkiss, I had not cut the mustard.

So I went home for spring break and got the letter that told me I had failed. I'll never forget that letter. It was from my English teacher, who was also my house master—another teacher who had a big influence on me. He told me he didn't think I was a quitter and that the whole faculty would like to see me pass that course.

At first, I didn't know what he meant, but when I went back to school they said to me, "If you take calculus as a fifth course next semester and pass it, we'll give you whatever grade you get on the final." That was an extraordinary exception on their part. They really took a leap of faith with me. Failing that course had been a culmination of all the math problems I had had in my whole life, and these guys weren't ready to put a fork in me and say I was done. It was a lot to ask of me academically, but I was very willing to do it. So outside of my regular courses, I had a tutor work with me in math, and I took the final again.

Because I hadn't taken that final when college acceptances came out, I couldn't get into any schools—they needed that grade. So everybody got their college acceptances at their mailbox one day, and I was accepted at no colleges. If I failed that test, I basically was not going to go to college. It really came down to that.

On the morning of the test, I remember thinking that I could just choke. In fact, most of the people in my class knew that college was coming down to this test. At breakfast they were saying, "Here we go . . ." When I came out, everybody asked, "What happened, what happened?" The professor corrected it within four hours, so right away I knew I had made it. As it turned out, passing that test got me into Princeton.

I'll never forget that letter from my house master, my English teacher, telling me that I had failed math but giving me that second chance. I'll never forget that.

What do you think about recommending prep school to others?

Even though prep school was a fabulous experience for me, it's such an extraordinary living environment for a kid that if the kid isn't right, it could be one of the worst decisions you ever make. You're isolating yourself from your family, and you're getting yourself in a very intense academic and athletic situation. You have to be almost on a "mission"—really driven—for the right reasons, too. I saw a lot of people driven for the wrong reasons at this school.

When I think of my not getting into any schools the day of

school acceptances, I felt a sense of vacancy, but I wasn't crushed. In my mind I already thought, "Well, I'll just go home. I know the guy at Westchester Community College, and I'll go to that junior college and play basketball there."

But I don't know what drove some of the other kids, maybe their parents, maybe just the feeling they had to do something for whatever reasons. I saw kids crying at their mailbox because they didn't get into Harvard. They got into Yale; they got into Princeton or Williams or Amherst; but they didn't get into Harvard. I just couldn't conceive of that, that a kid could be crushed because he didn't get in somewhere. And when you're at a school with kids who feel that way, who are so driven that not getting into one or two schools is a disaster—let alone not getting into college at all—that's when I realized that people who don't really have their heads screwed on straight in terms of "who they are" and "where they're going" are in big trouble. It's a very dangerous place for a kid like that: he might get run over or he might get taken for a bad ride.

I'd recommend it for a kid who is plugged in, who knows what he wants to do and has a sense of himself or herself. But I'd be extremely wary of sending my children to a place like that if I didn't think they were right for the prep school environment. If I could judge that.

At this point Terry and I talked at length about his college basketball career. In his senior year he was elected co-captain of the team, and he won several games with clutch shots in the last seconds. In another area of college life, however, Terry found it difficult to apply the same kind of passion he displayed on the basketball court.

The academic side of Princeton was the most disappointing thing about my whole experience. When I look back on it now, it's something that still bothers me. I would have thought, coming off prep school, that I'd be on an academic high that would have lasted me, enthusiasm-wise and effort-wise, the rest of my life. I mean I was hooked on academics. I thought that if I applied myself, people out there would help me the way my teachers had helped me at prep school. It was just so rewarding to be with good people and to study things that you like. I had the feeling that Princeton was going to be the time to really enjoy my studying and also play some basketball, which I loved. I wasn't even required to take math.

Academically, however, I just didn't meet the people that I met at prep school. I mean, I was psyched to study at Hotchkiss, but I also got plugged into some real good people. I sat in the classroom with only four or five other people, and we would have a teacher we could really talk to, and he could get to know us. Maybe that's why I really liked it. When I got to Princeton, there were no people at the other end.

I worked real hard my freshman year and did pretty well. I got three B's and a C, which was okay for me. I was really playing basketball hard, and socially I was starting to go out and do things a little more than I had when I was in high school. But all of a sudden I started to feel like I wasn't enjoying the academic side. I didn't know my professors, and the assistants who taught the small group courses were often people I could not relate to at all. I don't mean to say this in a prejudicial sense, but for two straight years I had homosexual tutors. The biggest thing on their minds was gay rights, and they openly talked about that. I got along with them, but I just didn't warm up to them as people.

And most of my courses were huge. When I'd go into a lecture, it was like I was one of several hundred people. And I just wasn't getting excited about those classes; the reading lists looked like big blots of books instead of things I really wanted to read. I thought, "There's no way I'm going to read all this with basketball and everything else. I have four courses like this and fifteen papers to write." So I felt kind of defeated. I started to develop the attitude that I was just doing my work to get it done. That was horrible . . . and each year it got a little worse. Basketball became more of an emotional outlet for me—the centerpiece of my life at college.

So there I was, two years into college, thinking, "I'm at Princeton and academics just don't mean that much to me. I'm doing it, but I'm not really psyched about it." And my grades became mediocre. I even had a problem with a couple of courses that I shouldn't have had problems with just because I got a little lazy and a little uninterested. In my mind I figured I was mature enough to know what was important to me. It didn't seem to bother me then that I wasn't doing that well in school because I was enjoying myself and growing in other areas. I had a girlfriend at a nearby school, and I still loved playing basketball. Certainly something was going to suffer, and I chose to let academics suffer.

That bothers me now—it really does. Basketball evaporated after college, as I knew it would, but I figured I had to enjoy that as long as I could. And I'm glad I did, but that's gone. But the things that you learn through academics—they're the things that you carry with you. And I know I didn't give it my best shot in college.

Anyway, after college, in terms of a career, I just saw this huge void out there. My father was a lawyer, and I decided I didn't want to do that, even though I liked the way he seemed to reach out to people with what he did. Some clients who really needed it—he took care of them for nothing. But I also saw that he had to spend a lot of time writing at a desk or going down to the courthouse to find out how to get something done. He wasn't able to spend as much time with clients as I once thought he did.

I had no business experience either, except for working as a teller in a bank one summer and working for a sports network during another summer. But I figured coming out of Princeton, with the discipline of having been an athlete there, I had as good a shot as anybody else to get into the business world somewhere. I knew the way the world worked enough to know that there were a lot of misconceptions about the Ivy League—that other people who had A's at small colleges wouldn't get the same chances I would. That probably wasn't fair, but I figured I'd get a chance in business and do whatever I could with it.

My senior year I went through the interviewing process and got turned down by most of the people, but I did get a job offer from Manufacturers' Hanover in their training program. And I was very intimidated by it. I knew that I hadn't studied real hard—that frightened me—and I also knew the job would have a lot of math, which was still a disaster for me.

So I figured, this is going to be a real slap in the face in the adult world. But I've got to do it—I've got to find out a lot of things about myself. So I accepted the offer and was pretty nervous about it. I graduated and closed the book on college with that empty feeling academically, figuring that maybe I would go back to school way down the road. But right then I felt I should just go out there and get my behind whipped a little bit in the business world, find out what I'm all about.

A week after I graduated, I was back home with my family and I got a call from a headhunter who said he had talked to my basketball coach and got my name and wanted to talk to me. He asked me, "Do you know anybody who fits the following description: 'An athlete who is quantitatively oriented, did well in math and economics, and wants to make a whole lot of money in the business world?'" In retrospect, I realize he was asking me to put myself in there, but I didn't know that. I mentioned a guy who lived in Delaware, and I even offered to get his phone number. I also said, "I'm an athlete, but I'm not any of those other things." So then he said, "Well, wait a second, wait a second here. I think I'd like to talk with you a little further about it. Why don't you meet me at the Waldorf-Astoria tomorrow? All right?"

So I went down there and met this guy at the Waldorf. This job was in the brokerage business, and the recruiter said, "I think that you could do this job, and there's a lot of money involved in it. This firm is based in California, and I think it would be an interesting match, possibly. If you want to go to California in the next month or two, you can interview with the people out there. Why don't you check it out? I think it would be worth your while."

This was at the bottom of the market in 1981, so people weren't dying to get into the brokerage business. My only experience with a brokerage business had been with an older friend of mine from high school days—he was a broker. And I ended up having a friendship that wasn't as genuine as I thought it was. So my image of a broker was not very good, but I figured I'd check this thing out. My best friend from high school had a little extra money, and he offered to pay for my trip out to California. He said, "I want to get away, and we can go together. What the hell—we'll go and have a good time."

The interview was kind of a sideline thing, really. In fact, when I went for it, I had my bathing suit on underneath my business suit. I swear to God—I went into this office on Rodeo Drive, and I had a blue blazer on and my shorts and everything underneath it. All I kept thinking about was that my friend was waiting for me out in front, ready to go to Zuma Beach. As I went in, he said, "Hurry up and get it over with!" He wanted to get to the beach by noon.

So I went into this interview very relaxed because I had Manufacturers' Hanover in the bag. I talked with the guy who ran the trading operation, which was a really intense setting—everybody was yelling and screaming. This guy who was the head of the whole thing was talking about how much money all these people make, trying to impress me on that level. I really had doubts about the whole thing.

Then I went upstairs to interview with the guy who hired the headhunter; I think that's what turned everything around. He was a guy who had played ball in college, and we immediately had a lot in common. He wanted to get some basketball players in from good schools—his type of guys.

We really had a great interview. And a day or two later, when I was back home, they called me and said they'd like me to work for them. Now, I didn't even really know what it was all about except that it was going to be a training program. Supposedly, after a year I'd be exposed to the business enough so that I could decide what area I'd want to be in—whether it would be as a trader, a salesman, or an analyst. There were also some other areas that I didn't even know existed at the time: venture capital, investment banking, underwriting—I didn't even know what a stock was. These guys didn't know that, though. They didn't even know I had had trouble with math my whole life, and here I am supposed to be dealing with figures and numbers. They just said, "You know, you've got all these things open to you. You just go through the training program. We'll get you registered, and you'll see what's up after that."

So this is one of those examples where they were buying the Ivy League. I was a nice guy and I got along with this guy, and he figured I would definitely do well in this business since I was from Princeton. I don't know why he thought that, but that's what he wanted to think.

I felt very lucky to have gotten that offer since Manufacturers'

Hanover had me a little scared. I figured, "If I take this I'll definitely get some business experience, and what the heck—they're paying me a pretty decent salary."

The whole thing turned out to be crazy; I had some incredible experiences there. I found out that the business world was very different from what I thought it was. I used to think it was this mysterious system where everything was very complicated—that there were all types of strategies and consulting things that went on at a high level intellectually. I found out it wasn't that way at all. Most of what went on, especially in the business I was doing, was transaction oriented; everything was geared toward getting a trade done.

All the research and academic work was done by people who were academic-research types. Everybody else was either a trader or a salesman in my business. And all they cared about was making the buck, making the transaction.

I found out it was very shallow. The mentality was, "Just get the trade done. Nobody cares how you do it. Get it done, and smooth it over with your customer however you have to—just make sure we can continue to do business." There were a lot of things that were ignored, like ethics and a real interest in customers. Nobody thought about whether something was good for the customer.

The more it went on, the more I realized that this was just a business for people who really wanted to make a lot of money. That's all that mattered. Even the guys who were doing the analytical work were constantly being pressured to bend their work here and there to try to make trades happen. And I saw that it took a very big toll on a lot of these guys . . . I saw what it did to a lot of people's lives.

I tend to look at people down the road. When I was a freshman in basketball, I would look at seniors and project what it would be like to be there and ask myself, "Are they doing something I'd like?" Well, when I would look at thirty-five or forty-year-old guys in the brokerage business, the first thing I'd see was that there weren't many of them. For whatever reason, a lot of them were gone, and those that were left seemed to have gone through a lot of trouble in their lives.

After I was in L.A. for only two weeks, they moved a forty-year-old guy from their Chicago office to the L.A. office. A very, very nice guy. His relationship with the Chicago office manager had not been good, so they moved him to cover L.A. accounts and to get him away from that guy. He moved into the apartment complex where they had me living, and he left his family back in Chicago.

More and more I could see that a lot of bad things that happen to people in this business were happening to him. We had to be at work every morning at 5:00 A.M., so my usual routine was to go by and get him at 4:30, and we'd go to work together. After he was there about a week, I went by his door one morning. A knock on the door. No answer. Finally I just went to work and called him all that night. No answer. The next day I tried him again without any luck. Finally, by the end of the work day I was really concerned and I called the guy who ran our department. He said, "Why don't you come upstairs?" So I went upstairs, and he said, "Look, we've had a little incident with George. You seem to have gotten close to him. Maybe you could help us out here."

He went on to say, "I just fired him. He's had a drug problem for the last couple of years, and he's gone up and down in this business. With his good years, he's done well; in some bad years he's been through a couple of firms, and he's just run his course at our firm, I think. So I just fired him. But the only problem is that when I called him to tell him he was fired, he answered the phone and said that he was hurting real bad—that he had overdosed on some drugs. I think he was saying that for sympathy because he didn't want to get fired. But, to cover my bases, when you go home this afternoon, would you do me a favor and just stop by there and see if he's okay?"

So I thought to myself, "These guys *really care*. They don't even try to see if he's telling the truth. They're going to wait six hours and have me do it." When I got home I went over to his apartment and knocked on the door. He answers the door with a drink in his hand; the shades are drawn, he has sunglasses on, and he can barely walk. It turns out he *had* taken a drug overdose, and he really was in bad shape. He couldn't feel his legs, and he'd gone to the bathroom all over himself. So I took him to the hospital and called his wife in Chicago and told her he was okay, but she'd have to come down. It was a long night.

I guess there's just built-in people problems in this business. Everybody's so driven to make the money, which is tremendous money, but it's not guaranteed year in and year out. You're a hero one year and the next year you're a dog. A lot of the guys can't handle that; they'll make $400,000 one year, and the next year the same accounts that loved them now hate them because they "bagged" them in ten stocks. But they were *forced* to bag them. If they didn't bag them, the firm would give the accounts to somebody else. I just remember seeing guys who made a lot of money and thought they were on top of the world and then the market went down and they ran into these troubles.

Some guys can just handle it, for whatever reason. They're survivors, and they end up being partners. They're the "winners," if you want to use that term. But they're the winners through attrition. I just looked at it and thought to myself, "What's the best-case scenario here? I'm maybe once again lucky in my life, and I'm the guy who survives all this. But even if that's the case, is that what I want to be? Do I want to be just a survivor? Do I want to survive in this business to make that big hit and be like the guy in the firm who makes the biggest money? Am I going to look at him and say I want to be like him because of his money and because he lives in an incredible place? I can't say I want to be like him because his accounts love him, and he's a good guy, and he's good to other people here. I can't say that this is a great place to work and everybody here is really good to everyone else. I can't wait to be forty here."

It was more like, "If I survive here, I'll have a lot of money. And then the other part of my life will be nicer because I have a lot of money." But then I also realized that the hours were just long enough where I wouldn't even enjoy that part of my life. In other words, I realized I could be my friend in the apartment without even realizing it. It might sneak up. Maybe he didn't know what was really happening. Maybe the first night in the hospital was when he first realized that he was so messed up. And that was possible because he was a really good guy, but he had just been through the ups and downs of this business. Even with all this thinking, I still figured that I didn't know enough about the business yet. I was up in the air about the whole thing.

After nine months I had to pick what I wanted to do, and I decided to be a sales trader. Intellectually and socially, I knew I could do every part of the job. It was pretty superficial, really, just calling people up and reading off names of stocks that were being traded. But I didn't think I could do any of the other jobs and be effective, nor was I really interested in them. So I chose sales trading and asked to go back East. They moved me to Philadelphia and gave me a list of accounts to cover. I was off and going, and it was "fish or cut bait." I guess what unfolded in the next eight months really taught me a lot about where I stood with this whole thing.

Actually, I guess it wasn't all bad; there were some rewarding things that happened. By getting to cover accounts, I was able to talk with people outside of our firm, and I started to make some friendships, which were really nice. I wasn't really helping them that much, because as a broker you trade for them or you do transactions for them—but they could do it with anybody. So you don't feel you're doing anything extraordinary for them. But at the same time you take them out socially and you get to know them. I made a couple of really good friendships, and I at least felt I was doing something; I wasn't a trainee any more.

But when I got to know the three people I worked with in the Philadelphia office and some other people in the business, I came to realize that I had very different values from these people. When you work close to people, you understand their motivations; you realize what they're up to. For example, one of the guys I worked with, who made a couple hundred thousand a year, would openly brag about how he cheated on his wife, and he would bring girlfriends into the office. One time he asked me if I would leave early before a holiday so he could use the office to fool around with his girlfriend. Then his wife would come in to visit him a week later and I'd have to make like nothing happened.

It was just not my style. I would much rather have worked with people that were good at their work and liked it, but who didn't spill their outside life into work like that. And here he was—he's celebrating his sex life, his extramarital affairs. They were all part of my going to work every day. One of the other fellows who worked with me was basically the same way; he started having an affair with somebody else from our office. Work got to be pretty crazy; and I felt cheapened by working with these guys, but I didn't think it was up to me to pass judgment based on my morals or my feelings. That's none of my business, so it wasn't going to make me leave my job. Wherever you go, you're going to have to work with different types of people.

But I guess the thing that brought matters to a head came when my firm screwed one of the friends I had developed among my accounts; and I ended up screwing him without even realizing it. This was an older guy who I got to know socially, and he seemed to like me. He did business with me for all the stupid reasons that people do business with other people: I was a jock and we were both Irish. It's very stupid, but at the same time, that's the way things work.

I felt some warmth for the guy; he was a good guy. And he started just giving me business. I had a couple of months where I did $30,000 worth of business with him; that was $4,000 of commissions in my pocket for one month. And that was just from one account! He was just giving it to me. You can see how this business can get pretty incredible; you couldn't ask for a better scenario than the one I had with this guy.

Over the next two or three months some things happened with his case: my firm "fronted" some orders that I was doing for him. I'll explain. The job of some guys in L.A. was to buy and sell stock with only the firm's money. They weren't doing what I was doing— selling or soliciting orders from the outside. They were speculators, short-term traders, who were looking to make money any way they could. And one of the ways they were making money was "front running" orders of accounts. These guys controlled everything, so when I would come across the speaker system with an order to buy stock, guys who I had worked with in L.A.—I thought I knew these guys—would hear me come in with the order.

One time I was going to buy stock for this friend of mine, and when I announced it, my firm ran down there and bought it ahead of us and then charged a higher price to sell it. I was naive to the fact that the L.A. guys were doing this; my friend thought it was us, but he couldn't prove it, so he let it go.

The next time around it was the guy in my office who cheats on his wife who did it to us. He had a seller of the stock that I was looking to buy for my same friend. My friend confided in me that he wanted to buy forty thousand shares, and he asked me if I could find out how much the seller had. If my seller had forty thousand, he'd buy it, but if he didn't, he wouldn't buy unless all of it was bought by somebody else. It was a perfectly legitimate way to protect himself so the stock price wouldn't get pushed down after he bought it.

I went to the guy I worked with—this guy right across the desk from me. I'd worked with him for six months; I'd met his family; I'd seen him cheat on his wife. I should have known better then, but I said to him, "I've got to know exactly how much you've got for sale because I won't be able to do this unless I know." So he said, "Give me a minute," and he came back and told me, "Look, it's fifty thousand shares for sale, but the firm will buy the other ten thousand so there'll be no stock hanging over the market. It'd be a great deal for him. Tell him we'll sell him forty thousand and we'll buy the other ten." So I called my account and told him that. Long story short, it turns out that the seller had a hundred and twenty thousand for sale; sixty thousand sat on the market, and the stock went down three points in two days. My firm and I had bagged my friend. But I honestly didn't know. I had no idea.

My friend did find out this time, and he said, "How am I supposed to do business with you if you don't know what's going on?" But he was good about it, and later he asked me to buy some shares again. Same story. My firm bought the same shares first and ran the price up a point and a half and then had the gall to turn around and ask him if he'd buy it at that point.

Well, my friend slammed the phone down on me during that conversation, and I don't blame him. I didn't hear from him again for two days, and I finally took the initiative and asked if I could come over and see him. When I went up to his office and walked in the door, everybody at that organization just stopped and looked at me like I was the lowest form of human life . . . and I realized that I really was.

I'd never felt like that in my life. My firm was doing it, but I was part of it. You know, I'd always been a part of something I felt good about—my family or my team or something else. But here I was with a great opportunity to make money and I felt like crap. The fact that I didn't know about it didn't make any difference. I did it. And the guys I worked with—it was like being a part of a band of thieves. Their idea of making money also meant screwing over certain customers. In this case, it happened to be mine.

My friend was still pretty nice about the whole thing under the circumstances, but he did say things about my firm that I could not deny. He was right; I knew he was right. He was absolutely *one hundred percent* right.

For me this was the culmination of things. Right there. I went home that night—it was a Friday—and called my parents to tell them I was quitting. My father said, "Are you sure you know what you're doing" I said, "Yeah." He said, "Okay, then do it."

I went back Monday morning and quit. Forget it, over with. They were shocked. They said, "Fly out to L.A., we want to talk to you about it. What are your reasons and everything?" And I didn't even tell them my reasons because I knew they wouldn't change, and it would get around the street that I was trying to make some moral issue of the whole thing. I just told them I had personal reasons and decided I didn't want to be a part of the business. So they gave me two weeks to think about it, and I stayed for that time. Then after two weeks I quit. That was it. I didn't have a job or anything . . . I just left.

How did you feel walking out the door the last day?

I didn't know what I was going to do, which was a little unsettling. And the fact that I had gotten that far along in the whole thing kind of bothered me. I felt very confused. For the first time in my life I wasn't really sure about a lot of things, or about myself either. Other times when I had just let things happen, there always seemed to be a happy ending. But for the first time, what happened wasn't that great. I know I did the right thing to get out, but I felt a certain emptiness, for sure.

I had some money saved so that wasn't a problem, but that whole period was a very tough time in my life. I didn't even make a move for the first three months because I didn't know where I wanted to start. I really had tremendous misgivings about getting back in the brokerage business, and I went back and forth five or six times as to whether or not it would be a smart move.

I realized there certainly were firms that do business a lot better. But I also had to decide whether or not there were things about the brokerage business in general that were wrong for me. In other words, "Why was it that so many people didn't feel upset about certain things, and I did?" Maybe that should have told me that I wouldn't be happy even at another firm.

I was twenty-five at the time, and I figured I should make a decision to get in or get out. But if I wanted to get out, I didn't know what else I could do.

I spent three months just thinking about that. And I probably read more in those three months than I ever had in my whole life. I got back into being more academic about things, and I regained the vigor toward studying that I had lost when I was in college. I just read everything I could get my hands on, and talked to a lot of people—I guess introspection is the best word for the process I was going through. That's when I really started to think about getting a graduate degree and becoming a teacher. My gut was starting to tell me that that's where I wanted to go. And I'm still at that point now. I'm following my gut. But I'll be damned if I really know.

There have been practical decisions since that point. I realized that if I wanted to get a graduate degree, it would be smart to pay for it with my own money instead of borrowing any more than I had. So I interviewed and got back in the brokerage business on the sales side instead of the trading side, which is a little more sane. And I started going to graduate school at night about a year ago. It's going to take me about two and a half years to do it, but my instincts are telling me I would be happy as a teacher-coach.

My first feeling out of college was that I'd overdosed on basket-ball, and I probably needed some distance from it. I think if I went right into coaching and teaching, which was a thought in college, I would have felt that I never really knew what else was out there. I might have been frustrated by a life without money or material things. And now I don't have that feeling. I don't have that feeling at all.

If I'd found something in business that I loved, the trappings of money and material things would have just come with it. And then I probably would have graciously accepted that, tough as it would have been, let me tell you. But I can say that I've had experience in the business world, and it certainly wasn't fulfilling. The money that was starting to come didn't seem to make that much of a difference. Although I guess if there were a box and I had to check "money problems" or "no money problems," I'd check "no money problems." I'd take the money because when I had it, it was nice not having to worry about bills or financial pressures. But I realized that the more important thing for me was the absence of money problems rather than an excess of money. I'd seen people who made a hell of a lot of money whose lifestyles didn't get me all that excited.

One of the things that pointed me toward teaching and coaching was that I still have some of those same feelings about basketball that I had in college, although I don't think about the game as a player. In fact, when I play now, I'm terrible. I'm horrible. I really degenerated fast. I now realize what an overachiever I was, but it's just that I still love the game. I honestly do love it. It attracts a type of person that is a lot—well, like me, and I can relate to it.

And then the other side is that I would like to reach out to people, and coaching would certainly be one way to do it. I would never want to coach on the business level, which is what I think college basketball is on. I might as well be a broker if I do that. They're just trading players in and out. That's all they do: bring in one player, send out another; find an alum—tap him for his money potential. But I like the high school or prep school level, where I could really be a part of kids' experience.

I do admit to some reservations about the lifestyle and the parochial mindset at those small schools. It would have to be the right school, if I'm lucky enough. And it would also be difficult financially if I didn't get a little ahead of the game now from this brokerage business. There might be some time down the road when I'll have to face that. So there are definite little fears I have. But for me those are better trepidations to face than the land mines that come with the money in the brokerage business. I just figure that nothing's perfect—there is no Camelot. I'm following my gut, and my gut says to get my master's degree now and see if that's right. So far, I'm definitely excited by the track I'm on now.

Down the road, though, I'm also looking forward to meeting somebody and having a family of my own. I'm excited about that as much as anything. And I'm sure if I find someone with the same outlook I have, teaching at a prep school would be a great life. But it wouldn't be nice to be at a prep school with somebody who didn't want to be there or if I were alone. At this stage of my life, I almost feel happy that I'm in the brokerage business and going to school because the timing works out right. I've got this business in perspective: I'm making enough money to finance school and live, and I still have opportunities to meet a lot of people. So I'm set for at least the next year or two, and looking ahead—yeah, I'm psyched.

―――――――――――

As I drove toward the Procter & Gamble building on a gray, mid-winter morning, I felt a certain kinship with Terry Ryan. Unaccompanied by any feelings of purpose and self-fulfillment, the idea of making an ever-increasing amount of money did not hold much interest for me, either.

But such sentiment was a secondary issue as I headed toward a meeting with my boss and her boss on the day after I had walked off my job. More than anything else that morning, I was scared. I was about to admit that I would not fulfill a number of people's expectations of me: my bosses', my parents', my own.

As the meeting began, I felt I was at some kind of corporate execution. In a small, sterile-looking conference room, I sat with my back to the wall and my fists clenched around the arms of a metal chair. My two bosses sat opposite me, in front of the door. I couldn't bring myself to face them. I looked down at the floor or stared at a space between them as they asked questions and I whispered back.

"Ideally, what would you like to do, Andy? Do you know?"

"Somehow . . . I'd like to do something that reaches out to other people—that touches their emotions."

"What about your job?"

"I don't think I want to go back."

There was a quick phone call to the personnel office. Then my boss took a deep breath and said: "We wish you had approached us sooner, but we do accept some of the responsibility for what's happened. When the company decides it wants someone, we recruit very hard. But we only go after people when we think there's a good fit for them, as well. Since that doesn't seem to be the case here, we can arrange for you to go on a 'special assignment.' Your salary will continue for a period of time, and, basically, your job will be to figure out what you want to do next. You can even see a career counselor at our expense, if you'd like."

I nearly fell out of that metal chair. P&G gave me a new life.

QUESTIONS, QUOTATIONS, AND EXERCISES

GENERAL:

    a.   What incidents, images, ideas, or words from this chapter stand out for you?

    b.   When were you happy, sad, or mad as you read it?

    c.   What advice would you like to have given Terry?

    d.   What are the lessons for your life?

FOCUSED:

"In retrospect, I know it was a decision of major importance, and I can honestly say that there was very little calculation in it."

    a.   Think about three major decisions you have made in your own life. What kind of calculation went into them? What are the pros and cons of your approach?

    b.   What makes for a "good" decision?

    c.   Think about some upcoming decision. How can you increase your odds of making a good decision?

"I tend to look at people down the road. When I was a freshman in basketball, I would look at seniors and project what it would be like to be there and ask myself, 'Are they doing something I'd like?'"

    a.   As you look down your present road, who is doing something you might like to do? What did he or she do to get started?

   b.   How does it feel when you project yourself a few years down your present road?

   c.   What other roads do you want to investigate now?

"I'd never felt like that in my life. My firm was doing it, but I was part of it. You know, I'd always been a part of something I felt good about—my family or my team or something else. But here I was with a great opportunity to make money and I felt like crap. The fact that I didn't know about it didn't make any difference. I did it."

   a.   When have you felt badly about something in which you were involved?

   b.   How would you evaluate your current activities from an ethical viewpoint?

   c.   What does the above analysis suggest?

"But I realized that the more important thing for me was the absence of money problems than an excess of money. I'd seen people who made a hell of a lot of money whose lifestyles didn't get me all that excited."

   a.   If you had a lot more money, what would you do?

   b.   If you had a lot less money, what adjustments would you make?

   c.   What does the above tell you about your real priorities in life?

The Same God

O N A NIGHT IN EARLY JANUARY I was expecting *the* phone call. Two days earlier I had sent my parents a rough draft of the Terry Ryan story. This would be their first glimpse at something solid from this nebulous book idea; and I desperately needed their support and encouragement if I were going to move further along the precarious limb onto which I had already, tentatively, stepped. But my parents had heard some far-flung ideas from me before that had never materialized. And, besides, they're not the kind to gush with enthusiasm over a highly speculative project.

I came home from work and saw the red light flashing on my answering machine. I rewound the tape and heard my father's voice:

"Andy, this is your father . . ."

I know, I know.

"Your mother and I have both read your story, and we can see one big problem . . ."

I stopped breathing.

"We don't see how you can possibly find other stories as good as this one."

All right! And I punched the air like a boxer.

In January I was also hard at work on my "special assignment" at Procter & Gamble. My job was to find another job, and every day people around the office would ask questions about my search and try to give me encouragement: "You'll have no problems—not with a Harvard MBA and P&G on your résumé. What are you looking at, anyway?"

Since everyone expected that I would merely switch to another lane of the fast track, I could not bring myself to mention my book idea as a legitimate option. Even I recognized that the odds were stacked against an inexperienced writer getting something, anything, published—and that I would almost certainly need another way of supporting myself.

So one of the things I did was contact an executive recruiter in Connecticut who specializes in placing consumer marketing people. "Maybe I would like marketing better at a different company," I thought, "One that's smaller, less intense, closer to home." Certainly I felt that I should not ignore my background and training.

This recruiter was a crackerjack. Within a week, she hustled up three interviews with leading companies. One of them looked particularly interesting, Cadbury Schweppes, a company in Connecticut that makes candy and soft drinks, products that might be more fun to market than laundry detergent.

There seemed to be a mutual attraction between myself and the people at Cadbury. Naturally, everybody was skeptical as to why, if I were really interested in marketing, I would want to leave P&G. But within ten days I found myself having breakfast in an executive dining room with a marketing vice-president. If I sold him, I knew I would be offered an attractive job in line with my training and salary history—and, in Scott Harris' words, "in sync with my Ivy League background."

Selling myself came naturally for me, as it does for many fast trackers. And I also had the advantage of having been a personnel manager prior to business school; I understood and appreciated the art of landing a job offer. Often a strong, positive statement delivered by the interviewee at just the right moment can clinch the deal.

As the waitress cleared our plates, such a moment arrived. The vice-president leaned forward and said: "I don't know what you're looking for, Andy, but I want you to understand that we pray to the same God as Procter & Gamble. We're a different size, and there are other differences, sure, but the differences aren't all that big."

I knew what was required. I had to lean forward in my chair, look directly at the vice-president, and say, "I understand where you're coming from, but I've done a lot of research and thinking, and I can honestly say that Cadbury offers *exactly* the kind of opportunity and challenge for which I've been searching. You guys have got some great action here, and I want a piece of it."

In that instant I knew that saying those words would probably mean giving up on my book idea. But with such an uncertain future for that project, with the odds so long for an unpublished writer, it seemed so much smarter to go for the sure thing. As my recruiter said, "You can explain away one screw-up on your résumé, but you can't afford another."

Nonetheless, I did not go for the sure thing; I did not sit up in my chair and say the right words. Prior to that Cadbury interview I had gained a fresh perspective on deviating from the fast track— on chasing one's dreams—from my sessions with a career counselor and from talking with Darnell Johnson, another Ivy League athlete whom I interviewed in January. Darnell was someone who had thought a great deal about chasing a dream of his own. In fact, he was still thinking about it when I talked with him.

The Wall Street Trader:
Darnell Johnson

"I think the essence of a life is to realize what
you are—and to follow that realization. I think I've
realized what I am. I've just continued to put off
moving in that direction."—Darnell Johnson

*I*N THE MAIN CORRIDOR *of a small high school in upstate*
New York, there's a picture of a ruggedly built, smiling young
man holding a football. The young man's name is Darnell Johnson,
and his picture hangs above the trophy case.

Darnell Johnson was a high school phenomenon. Not only was he
such a gifted running back that he attracted over two hundred college
recruiting letters, but he was also class president, the male lead in
every school play, and a straight-A student. On top of that, Darnell
attended Catholic Mass every day.

By the time he was fourteen years old, Darnell had certain career
goals firmly in mind. He felt destined to become a doctor and priest;
and he had a well thought-out plan to achieve that ambition. "Admit
it," he says with a sheepish grin, "when you sit in church every day
you have to think of something."

He would build a strong high school record so that a good college
would accept him; he would earn a football scholarship to spare his
mother the tuition expense; and he would go off to medical school right
after college. That was the plan Darnell formulated as a freshman in
high school.

Four years later, scholarship in hand, Darnell headed to a mid-

western university with a fine academic reputation and an ambitious football program—a big-time football program. And that's when things began to happen for which he had not planned.

Now, despite a successful career and a happy marriage, Darnell is still haunted by an old dream.

My freshman year of football didn't go as well as I would have liked. I felt like I could make a contribution to the team, but I didn't get much of a chance to play. At the end of the season, though, the coach told me that he thought I could be one of the top rushers in the conference next year and that things would work out well. He also said that I should just practice lightly during the summer; he knew I was a hard worker and he didn't want me to come back burned out.

The next day I was walking to a biology exam, and I happened to pass by the gym. One of the assistant coaches saw me and called out for me to come into the head coach's office for a few minutes. The head coach asked me to sit down. Then he said that after a lot of reflection he had decided that he would like me to go to school somewhere else, that he wanted to use my scholarship for another player.

I was shocked; I didn't know what to say. So I tried to make a deal with the man. I said, "Look, I like it here. I'll practice hard this summer, and I'll come back even better than you want me to be." He said, "No, I don't think you can be as good as I need you to be."

Right then I didn't want to get into a big fight with him because I knew that he could probably help me go to another school if I didn't act up. I said, "Well, what are we going to do about this?" He said, "I'll do my best to help you get into another school." I also asked him if he was going to call my mother and tell her about this. He said, "Yes, I'll call her this afternoon."

So I left the office and started crying and didn't know what to do. I felt out in the cold. I didn't know if he'd help me, but we had been friends during the year. Good friends. I thought that he'd at least try to help me with the school situation.

I went and took the exam and that turned out okay. But after I got out of the exam, it hit me and I started crying again. I was still upset when I called my mother at ten o'clock that night. I said, "Hi, how are you?" She said, "Fine, how are you?" I said, "Well . . ." She said, "Well, what?" I said, "Nothing, nothing at all."

Then my mother said, "No, I can tell, there's something wrong." I said, "Well, did he call?" She said, "Who?"

Then I thought, Man, this coach is a lot more dishonest than he seemed. Initially, one of the reasons I had gone there is because he had promised me a five-year scholarship so that I could space out my academic credits if I wanted to. Secondly, he had told me that even if I were injured or not good enough, I would never lose my scholarship. He said that to my mother and to my high school coach the night I signed the letter of intent. But it turned out that this coach was a real loser and just wasn't honest at all. He never even called my mother as he promised; I had to explain it to her.

In retrospect, I made a wrong decision about college; and that was the first real setback in my life. After it occurred I began to think about whether or not I wanted to have a scholarship hanging over my head again. I did get back in touch with some of the other coaches that had offered me scholarships, but when I applied and was accepted at Brown University, I just felt that it would be best to go there and become a regular student.

After I transferred, my perspective on football changed—it completely changed. As far as being a player, I was the best I ever was when I was a freshman in college. But football didn't seem that important anymore after I got to Brown. As soon as I walked on the campus and saw the library and the other facilities, I felt that I didn't need football anymore to make me happy. But I still thought I could compete successfully with the guys on the team and in the Ivy League; I didn't think there would be any questions about it. I was just hoping that it wasn't going to be too embarrassing for the halfback I would replace when I became eligible in my junior year.

Then when the coach didn't even pick me for the team in my junior year, I was flabbergasted. I knew that I was better than he realized, but it was embarrassing when my friends at school came up to me and asked, "How come you're not on the team? We heard you were so good."

So I decided to train very hard during the summer before my

senior year. I had some close friends on the team who encouraged me, and when I was running or lifting weights I would think about the coach and say to myself, "He's not going to beat me. He's not going to beat me."

At the end of the summer I called the coach, who turned out to be a really good guy, and convinced him to give me a special tryout. I went and gave it hell. And I did make the team.

That was one of the most important experiences in my life. There was a really special feeling on that team among the players, and the fact that I rushed for over a hundred yards in several games was the icing on the cake. Most importantly, I proved to myself that if I apply myself and really focus, I'm able to do whatever I want.

Off the football field, I loved Brown . . . I just really loved it. What I found most interesting was that for the first time ever my ideas mattered when I took a test. At first I thought it was silly because I was the one who was supposed to be learning rather than expressing my opinions to others. I didn't fully realize at the time that I was able to move beyond just giving back what teachers had told me. I felt very free, as though I could begin to mature and understand who I was.

I also felt as though there was a tremendous burden off my back. It was funny—when I first went to college I thought that I would have to become a doctor in order to be successful. But when I started at Brown I thought, "Brown is going to help me become a well-rounded person and become successful in whatever I want to do." It's strange, but I felt very comfortable, like I was on the right track.

The idea of becoming a doctor did remain at first, but the idea of becoming a priest fell by the wayside—not because I felt less inclined to go to church or to be a Catholic: I just didn't think I wanted to express myself in that way. That was the time I had my first serious girlfriend, and I started seeing that I would like to be married someday and that I would like to have some children.

Then in the middle of my junior year, the idea of becoming a doctor began to change. I just thought that there could be something else to do that would not require such a struggle. It really wasn't a good reason for giving it up.

When I look back on my life, I see myself as being focused at certain times and unfocused at other times—sort of sitting back and just letting things happen to me rather than making things happen for myself. Those years at Brown were very enjoyable—the best years that I've had. But they were also years where I was just floating and doing things because I liked them rather than doing them with a real purpose. I liked history so I majored in that, but I just did it because I liked it. I don't know if that's necessarily bad, but I think it threw me off-stride for a while and definitely diverted my focus.

I kept putting medicine on the back burner. I remember thinking, "Well, at least I'm having a good college experience." But after I made the football team in my senior year, I realized that I could do whatever I wanted to do if I gave it the right amount of focus. And by the time I graduated, I had decided that I really would like to become a doctor.

After he graduated, Darnell decided to stay at Brown for another year; he planned to complete the pre-med requirements and then apply to medical school.

I went back for the extra year and enjoyed that, but I started to get a little tired of school by the end of the year, and I still needed to go for another semester. I began to feel as though I was asking my mother for too much money. She had done enough for me, and I had no money myself. So where was I going to go? I decided to work for a year or two before resuming school.

I thought I would like to learn about something new during that period, and I had become more interested in understanding the economy. So I thought that I might go off to Wall Street and get any kind of grunt job, just so I could learn from the people there.

After I had taken the final exams for my special student year, I answered an ad in the career placement office from a small firm on Wall Street. A friend had worked there and seemed to enjoy it, so I went ahead and interviewed for the job.

I also interviewed with a pharmaceutical company for a sales position, and they made me an offer. The day before I was flying out to revisit this company and hear more about the details of their offer, the Wall Street firm called and offered me a job. They actually wanted me to start work the next morning; but I told them that I was flying out to talk further with the pharmaceutical company and that it seemed only fair that I go and hear what they had to say. The man who called didn't like that, and he started yelling at me over the phone. I couldn't believe that I was having an argument with the person who was trying to hire me. But I went ahead and took the job because I didn't think it could get any worse than that. It could only get better from there.

Starting out on Wall Street, I thought that I might be out of my league. The people at the firm were very intelligent and expressed themselves very clearly as to what they wanted from me. From the first day I realized that meeting their expectations would entail a lot of extra work on my part, not only in learning the business but also in developing a certain attitude. There was a feeling among these people that they all had to do well as individuals and as part of a team. And this was a turning point for the firm because it was trying to diversify its products and move into the big-time on Wall Street.

While I was rotating between departments during the initial six-month training program, one of the department heads, a very volatile guy, walked in one morning and fired someone who had been working at his trading desk for about six months—he just told him to leave. So he picked me out of the training classes and gave me a phone and a computer and told me to do whatever I could.

That was a lot of responsibility right out of the chute, but it be-gan to work out well enough so that he asked me to stay on permanently. I became a close friend of his, and I think that was when I started to gain the confidence that I would be able to accomplish something with the company.

I certainly didn't look upon my job as a temporary one, but I thought that I would go to school at night after a year to take my remaining pre-med requirements. And I did take a few courses, but it was very difficult going to school when your responsibilities are increasing at work. It was at that time that our firm brought on a high-powered trader in my area who is the best on Wall Street at what he does. And working with him required a lot more of my time.

So after that year I began to feel a little more comfortable with being on Wall Street, and I began to think that it was a reasonable career alternative. Even if I weren't able to work in medicine, perhaps I could contribute money to certain medical causes and keep in close touch that way.

As his firm has grown rapidly over the last six years, Darnell has become increasingly successful in a specialized and highly profitable area—and his compensation has risen accordingly. Darnell has also been happily married to a Wall Street lawyer for four years. To many of their friends, the Johnsons lead a charmed life. But as we kept talking, Darnell explored his feelings about the medical profession that still remain.

I know I would like the work involved with being a doctor. I know I would like it as much as I liked playing football or as much as I like to have a day of trading that goes completely well. But I think with medicine I'd also be able to reach out to people, to enable some people to live a happier life because they are free from their medical problems.

I've often thought that I would like to become a psychiatrist because I enjoy talking to people and trying to help them with personal problems. I think that a lot of personal problems are a function of chemical imbalances in the body, and going to medical school would help me develop a more sophisticated knowledge of the causes of certain problems. Something along the line of small-town family medicine where counseling is a big part of the practice—that is what I think I would like to do the most.

I don't see medicine as a big money-maker. I see it more as a middle-class existence where I could just be there when somebody needed me and where I could spend good quality time with people. I guess one could easily say, Why not become a family psychologist or a counselor or a personnel manager, something that wouldn't require all the training. But my interest lies in understanding the body and why it reacts to certain trauma and stimuli. I'm fascinated by this incredible piece of machinery. I can look at bond or stock or option trades and understand the subtleties at work there; but it's never as beautiful as what happens in the body to counteract some sort of trauma or outside force. It's just an incredible, incredible unit—and I would like to understand more about it.

So in my third year on Wall Street, after talking it over with my wife and both of our families, I made up my mind to leave the firm and attend pre-med classes at Columbia.

One afternoon, several weeks prior to the beginning of classes, I waited for the partner in charge of the equity department to leave a meeting so that I could tell him I was resigning. I waited and waited for this guy, and then I just thought, I'll talk to him in the morning. It had become so late in the day that I thought he wouldn't want to talk with me.

He didn't come in the next morning, so I didn't talk to him then, either. And I just began to think and think more about it . . . and I finally decided that I would put the whole thing off. And that's what I've done since. I've continued to put off making a final decision because there are a lot of other factors. There's the responsibility to provide; there's a responsibility to keep my marriage as it is, which is wonderful; there's a responsibility to make sure that I'm not doing something that's rash, that I'm not foolishly chasing a dream that I've had since I was younger.

In a personal sense I do think the sacrifices it takes to become a doctor would be worth it. My real concerns have more to do with those around me—my wife and those in our families. I often think about something happening to one of my sisters' husbands or my mother or one of my wife's parents. That's a young man's responsibility if something were to happen. Right now I know I can provide fully for one or two other people in a worst-case scenario. But I would feel very guilty and selfish if I were to go back to school for eight years and not be able to provide in such a situation. I know that might be just another excuse not to do it because, perhaps, unconsciously, I don't want to put up with the sacrifices. But it's a true concern, at least consciously, and that's one reason that's held me back.

There are also some positives about my work situation now as well; I'm not unhappy by any means. I've been so lucky to work with the best person in my field. I've learned so much, not only about investments, but also about developing your own ideas and your own point of view. He's a true intellectual, and he's taught me that it's important to cover every base in order to be truly great at anything, and he's instilled in me a lot of good habits. I've been the luckiest person on Wall Street, I think, to work with him; and I appreciate that, even though I might not always show it. And there's still a lot more I can learn from him.

It's also a nice feeling to be part of a winning team. The group I work with has never had a losing month. And in terms of feeling competent, I certainly feel as though I can easily go somewhere else and be in charge of a department. In fact, I've been asked to do that. But that is not very important to me. I can't really project myself into the future as the head of an equity department or even a Wall Street firm. I can see myself doing that, but I don't know if I would want to do it. That's one of the reasons I'm still considering medicine.

I'm also a little bit haunted by a lack of fulfillment in my work now. In fact, there was a day not too long ago when I was riding to work on the subway and my heart started pounding. Honest to God, I thought I was having a heart attack and that I was going to die right there on the train. That was not the case, but I remember the feeling that swept over me at the time. I felt I was going to die without having given back all that much to society.

So in the last couple months, I've decided that I'm going to donate more to certain causes as long as I'm able. In that way I feel a lot better about working where I do because it enables me to do things—like help a local soup kitchen put on a Christmas party for the homeless.

It's not as though I'm making a lot of money off pornography, but it's a struggle to not feel one hundred percent toward what I'm doing. I think the essence of a life is to realize what you are— and to follow that realization. I think I've realized what I am. I've just continued to put off moving in that direction. That's a sad commentary.

Do you have a timetable?

Yes, I've decided this will be the year when I'll make the decision. After this I'll be too old, and I'm sure that we'll want to start having children in the next two or three years. Once the children come, I will not go off and do something just for myself for eight years—that I won't do. So before we begin thinking seriously about having a child, I want to make the decision about medical school.

Maybe I'm just looking for a sign that's never going to come. I'm waiting for an angel to appear at the dinner table some night and tell me that I'd better go to medical school . . . or I'll never eat again.

After I walked away from my job at Procter & Gamble, unlike Darnell Johnson, I could not even make the claim that I realized "what I am." My résumé said one thing: future marketing executive. But some strange inner voice had rebelled against that notion. What really frightened me was that I had no idea how to sort out the conflict and make a good decision. What constitutes a "good" decision, anyway? Without some kind of personal vision or mission, I had no criteria for distinguishing among different options that presented themselves—and no path for searching out possibilities that were not readily apparent.

Looking back on that period of turmoil, I am very thankful for Procter & Gamble's commitment to their people. I cannot imagine another company going the extra mile the way P&G did in my case, particularly when I had just walked away from my job at a critical point in the life of a new product. Yet P&G gave me the time, resources, and support necessary for me to chart a new direction. Amazing.

Without question, the most important resource made available to me was George Dershimer, a consultant and career counselor. I cannot overestimate the value of the ten hours I spent across the table from George in the basement of his home. In a more methodical and system-atic way than I had dreamed possible, he and I began to unravel what I was all about. I made lists of everything—skills, interests, values, and motivations. George and I then refined those lists by examining them against another list—my most satisfying accomplishments—and find-ing the common themes. When we finished, I knew why P&G was not a good fit and what criteria I should address in looking for my next endeavor. Above all else, I wanted to do independent and creative work—to put my own stamp on something—and to reach out to others in some way.

The week after I conceived this new vision of myself, however vague, it flashed in my mind during the interview with the Cadbury vice-president. It kept me from leaning forward in my chair and saying the right words to get a job offer. I must admit, though, that I struggled to simply sit back when the key moment arose. I had conditioned myself to "play the game" for so long that it felt awkward to abandon the role of the eager, young fast tracker. But I let the moment pass.

Maybe I did not know exactly what I wanted to do in late January, but I had a better idea of what I did not want to do. Immediately after the interview, I called my crackerjack recruiter and told her that even if Cadbury made an offer, I would not be interested. I thanked her for her efforts on my behalf and actually had the nerve to mention my desire to write a book. Although supportive of me personally, she was not the first, and certainly not the last, to tell me how difficult it was to get a book published.

Because of the soul-searching with George, however, the dream did seem slightly less than foolish. And I meant to chase it . . . at least for a little while longer.

QUESTIONS, QUOTATIONS, AND EXERCISES
GENERAL:

    a. What incidents, images, ideas, or words from this chapter stand out for you?
    b. When were you happy, sad, or mad as you read it?
    c. What advice would you like to have given Darnell?
    d. What are the lessons for your life?

FOCUSED:
"Most importantly, I proved to myself that if I apply myself and really focus, I'm able to do whatever I want."

    a. Think about three times in your life when you have applied yourself and really focused. What did you learn about yourself, your strengths, and limitations?
    b. How focused are you now? How much are you applying yourself?

   c. What lies behind and underneath your current level of focus and application?

"But I think with medicine I'd also be able to reach out to people, to enable some people to live a happier life because they are free from their medical problems."

   a. What needs do you see among those close to you?
   b. What needs do you see within your community, school, and/or workplace?
   c. What needs do you see in the larger world?
   d. How do you see yourself responding to any of the above now and in the future?

"My interest lies in understanding the body and why it reacts to certain trauma and stimuli. I'm fascinated by this incredible piece of machinery. I can look at bond or stock or option trades and understand the subtleties at work there; but it's never as beautiful as what happens in the body to counteract some sort of trauma or outside force. It's just an incredible, incredible unit—and I would like to understand more about it."

   a. Name three things that truly fascinate you. What makes them so appealing to you?
   b. In what ways are you pursuing your interest in each of the above now?
   c. How might you more fully engage your interests now? In the future?

"Honest to God, I thought I was having a heart attack and that I was going to die right there on the train. That was not the case, but I remember the feeling that swept over me at the time. I felt I was going to die without having given back all that much to society."

   a. What message is your heart sending you now?
   b. How might you live differently based on your heart's message?
   c. What would you like to "give back" to society?

Stripped

RING. RING. I picked up the phone in my Cincinnati apartment. "Mr. Fleming, this is Judy calling from the furniture company. We spoke yesterday about your payment problems with the living room set you bought.

"I talked with my supervisor this morning, and she said you have a choice: you can either pay us $600 in the next three weeks or we can take away your furn—"

"Take it away."

My "special assignment" was over, and I was being stripped of more things than just my living room furniture. When I walked out of the Procter & Gamble offices for the last time, I no longer had my company badge, a sizable income, or an easy answer to the question: "What do you do for a living?" I could only manage to say, "I'm a wr . . . a wrrrr . . . a wriii . . . I'm self-employed."

I had good reason for such stammering. George Dershimer, my career counselor, had suggested I elicit some critical reaction to the Scott Harris and Terry Ryan interviews I had written. And he mentioned a writer-friend, Sarah Isaacs, whose husband happened to work in the publishing business.

Great, I thought, she'll recognize the potential of these stories, show them to her husband, and things will go from there. Other young writers may have to struggle, but not I. Fate is on my side.

I needed the help quickly, too. Unless I secured an advance from a publisher, my money would run out within several months.

So I gave Sarah Isaacs the two chapters, with no introduction or outline for the book. I did not have any vision I could offer other than the idea that this book would be a collection of stories about the career choices of some high achievers.

Sarah didn't call back as quickly as promised; and I became very anxious to hear the confirmation, the blessing, that I was certain she would bestow. Finally, two days later, I called her.

"Sarah, this is Andy."

"Hello, Andy. Sorry I haven't called. I have read your stories, and I've been trying to find . . . well, let me say this: I think you write fairly well; I think you can do it. But these stories—they went on for so long, and I wasn't sure why I was reading them. Your idea . . . I just don't think it's punchy enough."

"I see."

"I know how badly you want to write, and I hate to be the one to say these things. But, you know, it's really tough to get a book published—even for an established author."

"Well, I . . . ah . . . really appreciate your taking the time to read my stuff."

"No problem, happy to do it. I just hate to have to tell you these things. Oh, by the way, my husband's been real busy, so I didn't have him read your material. I'll just put it in the mail—"

"That's okay, I'll come by and pick it up."

I was crushed. Humiliated. And all I could think about was getting those stories out of Sarah's hands. I did not want her spending one more second handling my work, my dream.

At ten o'clock I drove out to the Isaacses' beautifully appointed home and retrieved my stories. Then I came back to my apartment, now with no furniture and little hope.

That night I lay awake wondering what the future held for me. More rejection? A return to the environment I had just left? Would I have to admit to my parents and friends and—worst of all—to myself, that I wasn't capable of becoming a writer? That I had been foolishly chasing a dream? And if I wasn't a writer, what was I?

There were so many questions for which I had no answers.

It was during this agonizing time in March that I began attending an evening Bible study group in my neighbor's apartment.

There I met Mike Sinclair, who had also worked for a corporate giant. Mike was convinced that he had found the right answers for some difficult questions in his career and in his life. And he was very willing to share his story.

The Corporate Man:
Mike Sinclair

"'We've offered you so many different possibilities.
The one option we can't offer you insist on having.
Are you prepared to leave the company?'
And I said, 'Yes.'"—Mike Sinclair

*T*HE FOUR HUNDRED PEOPLE *in the congregation stood up and began to sing, really sing. No organ; no muffled voices; no faces buried in hymnals—everyone knew the verses by heart and stood happily singing, smiling, and nodding to one another.*

As a visitor in the back pew, I could see Mike Sinclair a few rows ahead. Slightly under six feet tall, with short brown hair, glasses, and the wiry frame of a long-distance runner, Mike did not look old enough to have worked eight years with one of America's most respected corporations. But he exhibited the quiet confidence and poise of someone who could make it to the top of his field. Mike's attractive wife, Kim, stood on his right, but he had his arm stretched around the tall young man on his left, a new member of the church.

Mike Sinclair was a long way from the corporate office.

It's funny, I remember getting to the end of my college years at Michigan University and being shocked at the thought: "Now what do I do?" The road just suddenly ended. For the first time I had to make a decision that really meant something.

Fortunately the glee club director had taken a liking to me because I had worked hard in several club positions. He had some friends at LTC [Large Technology Company] who were recruiting managers, so I interviewed with them in the fall for their Detroit office. It was very disappointing when I got turned down; I really had my hopes up for LTC.

In retrospect, I think I turned myself down, by not being willing to play their recruiting games. They would promise that I'd have an answer on a certain date, and then they'd defer it. When they kept deferring it, I got angry. In fact, I wrote them a letter expressing my disappointment in them, and, needless to say, didn't get the job.

That episode ended in December, so I began spending some time in the college placement office, and I did start interviewing. I really didn't know what I wanted to do, although it seemed natural to go into banking—my specialty in economics was money and banking—so I interviewed with some banks. I signed up for as many interviews as I could, but nothing really came up as I neared graduation. Then the summer came, and I still didn't have anything.

Again, the glee club director was a big help. He said, "Mike, I have someone from LTC I'd like to have you talk to in Chicago. Detroit turned you down, but I think you're good." So he ended up writing the guy, and I followed that up. Eventually I landed an interview at a branch in Kalamazoo.

Before I had my interview there, I talked to some people about LTC in the computer area where my dad works, and we discussed the kind of things I could bring out in an interview. I remember a little bit earlier, a career counselor had seen me come in and prepare for interviews as I was going through school. He said, "I've seen people like you. I know where they end up. They get the good jobs." I wasn't so sure then, but he proved to be prophetic.

At Kalamazoo they would ask me questions like, "What do you think of LTC?" And man, I'd give them three or four things that were very current about LTC that really impressed them. It was the preparation that definitely gave me a chance at getting the job. But then I talked with their regional director of recruiting, and he said, "Well, we don't really have a job now for you. Why don't you call us in another couple of months and see if there are any openings." Another ploy LTC uses to see how determined you are.

During those couple of months I remember my mom saying to

me, "Mike, you seem unhappy." I was really distressed about not having a job, and I began wondering where my life was going. During this period, though, I did make some big decisions. I turned down being a Sears management trainee, and I turned down being an insurance salesman. Really you do start groping, though, and you're tempted to take just anything. But I think I was still looking for the security of working for LTC.

So I called the regional director after a couple of months, and he was impressed that I got back to him. He said, "Dayton, Ohio, has a position, Mike. We'd like you to go down there and talk with them."

Interviewing with LTC is really tough because the branches coordinate their own interviews, and they just expected me to appear one morning in Dayton on my own. It was a six-hour drive to go to Dayton, and I ended up spending my own money and staying in a Dayton hotel the night before. I remember being very nervous. I thought to myself, "I don't have a whole lot of really golden opportunities. Here I am at the second interview—I really made the trip—and LTC is serious about me. Man, wouldn't it be *great* to work for them?"

The night before, I practiced interviewing in front of the mirror. I was also sort of religious—I didn't attend church regularly—but I remember praying to God, and we "negotiated" on my terms. I asked Him: "If You give me this job, I'll really devote myself to You—maybe retire early at fifty-five—and really give back to You what You've blessed me with."

The next morning I was very high strung. The interview wasn't until one o'clock so I went to a Merrill Lynch office in Dayton and said, "I'm interested in buying LTC stock, and I wonder if you could give me an analysis of their company?" Little did I know that the company's stock sold at an incredibly high price. The guy saw right through that ploy, and I had to explain to him what I was doing. He said, "Oh, that's no problem. Let me just print out on the computer how we view LTC." So I looked at that and we talked about some current LTC issues.

Then the real interview went quite well—the guy was very impressed. I happened to say a lot of the right things. They were

66

looking for someone to get into the manufacturing end, and I expounded on the experience that I had working in a plant as a forklift driver—how I saw all the different work stations interacting together, how the waste from one is the input to another. I remember he asked, "What would you like to be doing in five years?" Something just came out of me, and I said, "I'd like to be sitting in your chair interviewing a young man to take on this position." I think that really struck him. So he told me at the end of the interview—"Mike, there's a 99.999% chance that I can give you this job. I want to give it to you. But I have to hold off for some clearances, and I'm not sure if we're talking October first. Probably by November, possibly by December, but no later than January will you have a position here."

I was just thrilled, and I remember feeling really close to God on that long ride home. My dad was still at work when I told him about this, and he said, "Well, what makes you so sure you have this job?" But I just didn't think anything could keep me from getting that job now. And they finally did offer me the job with a starting date of January 1. That was real exciting; there was no question on that decision.

One attraction of LTC was that I would start out at a level much higher than I would at other companies. I thought, "No, I don't want Sears management or these bank jobs—it's LTC. And from reading some magazine articles I also knew that LTC took very good care of their employees and that there was a lot of security there. But probably more than anything, I was attracted by the reputation, the allure—just that I would be working for LTC."

So they hired me as a systems engineer, and that was remarkable because I had no computer background. I think LTC was just looking for people with good communication skills who were ambitious, and who did extra things to make their mark; they could train people themselves. I was really in the same boat with everybody else they hired. It was good pay, and I was ready to go.

But there were a series of events in December that made it difficult to start with LTC. My long-time girlfriend, Sandy, and I had started dating again while I was back in my hometown; she was there student teaching. It had gotten rocky my senior year in college—she was dating some other people—but we had begun to renew our relationship. I didn't ask her to come down to Dayton with me, but I think I was tempted to ask that. Anyway, it ended up that she got married in December. Shock, shock.

So we were dating while she was engaged—for almost four months. And she just couldn't bring herself to tell me. I guess there was enough doubt in her mind about her marriage that she didn't know what to do. I was going away for Christmas vacation with my family, and at the last opportunity before I left she told me that she was getting married and just how difficult it was for her to give me this news and how much she had always dreamed of being my wife. It was a very emotional scene.

I guess my leaving town might have been a factor in her decision. She'd been dating this other guy—he had all the credentials in the world—and I guess she didn't want to risk not having someone, which is sad. And to me, emotionally, it was just heart-wrenching. I probably never cried as hard as I did then. I went off on Christmas vacation and then started work . . . and I didn't even know for sure if she ended up getting married. I called her mother to ask how the wedding was, thinking that was the most diplomatic way to find out. She said it was fine. And so I started at LTC at probably the lowest point in my life.

It was very difficult in Dayton, where I didn't know anyone. I'd never had a white-collar job before; computers were totally new to me; and I was often in the office by myself studying books. My phone *never* rang. I think LTC could have done some things to reassure new people better. I felt very empty and insecure, while everybody else was busy doing their thing.

I remember waking up in the mornings in a sweat. I had a lot of doubts about my own abilities with all the things that had come to a head—Sandy, a new town, a new position. You look at all the stress factors and they definitely added up at that point.

It took a few months, but I got through it somehow. I think one of the best things was going off to a five-week training class in Atlanta with a lot of other young LTC people who were in the same boat. But there was definitely pressure, which was intentional on LTC's part to see if you could handle things. The big one was that you had to make an eighty percent grade overall in the class. Otherwise, you go through the disgraceful situation of being sent back early—everyone in your office knowing, of course, that you didn't make it. They would usually give you a second chance, but if you failed that, you were told that there were places that would be better for you than LTC.

Gradually I grew more confident about my own ability to handle things at work. My security in life was definitely LTC, and I worked hard. I was willing to spend extra hours to do better, and I did reasonably well. I developed good communication skills and became known as a systems engineer who was good at the marketing side of things.

So I ended up spending five years in Dayton, and it was about three years into it that I think management started looking at me as a guy who had really grown a lot and who had management potential. I was ambitious about that, too. I thought, There's a lot that I have to learn, but it's worth it, and I want it.

It parallels my high school years in a way, with me thinking back then, Really man, are you going to do well academically or not? Here it was: Am I going to do well in my job or not? But as I got better at my job, just as I found after the A's started coming in school, I started to ask myself, Well, what else is there?

There was a little emptiness, or at least openness to other things. I remember coming home some times in Dayton thinking, This is a real rat race . . . Where is this leading to? And I remember mellowing out some nights and just listening to some music, not really feeling fulfilled. The questions kept looming: If I do well and I move on to the next position, what's that going to bring me that is different from what I have now? Yeah, I'll be more respected; yeah, I'll have more responsibility for people. Is that what I want?

And yet I didn't see any other options. I didn't feel I had the ability to just drop LTC and seek something else. Things were going well, and I didn't want to leave something good and not have a backup. That's why one of the most important things in my life—about three years into my job at LTC—was going to a company-sponsored career planning retreat.

I had been to some career planning seminars before and didn't really think this one would be very helpful. And yet it was. One instructor was really exceptional; his whole message was that you can plan to be happy. Happiness is something that can be attained; it's not just a vague ideal that hopefully you run into somehow. He said, "Really, to plan your career you've got to plan your life as well, because if you plan your career separately, you're never going to achieve your life goals. And aren't your life goals greater than just merely your career goals?" And he suggested that we go off on a weekend by ourselves and write down all of the things that make us happy.

So I ended up following his instructions and writing down fifty things that made me happy. I just opened myself up. I had run a little bit in college and had become a marathon runner in Dayton, so I wrote things like how I love to drink beer after a hard run. Or how I like sitting by a little stream and watching it flow down, just letting my mind wander. And I like to teach people, so I added that.

The next step was to transfer each of those thoughts onto a three-by-five card and prioritize what makes you the happiest. Then you write down how you spend your average day, time-wise. That's kind of tough, but you can make some guesses. Based on those things, you analyze where you would like to be spending more of your time.

For me, the happiest I'd ever been was when I felt close to God. When I won a prestigious music scholarship in high school and came home and watched the sun set, just being really at peace, I felt that God helped me with that achievement. And I thought about coming back from the interview with LTC, that long drive, and how I really felt that God had helped me because of my one intense prayer. It was really during the times of real, tangible success that I have felt close to God. As if He and I were relishing the victory.

A few months later, on New Year's Day, I was cross-country skiing out west, and it was a gorgeous day—crystal clear with bright, shining snow. And I looked back at the planning exercise I had just gone through and thought, God, I'm not really giving You much of my life. I want to seek a church where I can really grow. I want to know more about You. I want to be more pleasing to You. I didn't think I was disappointing, but looking at the way I spent my time and how He made me happy, virtually no time was given to Him. That really made an impact. I decided—doggone it, I'm going to find a good church and really commit myself more than I have in the past.

So I went back to Dayton and looked at different churches, and I found a Presbyterian one, very similar to the one in which I had grown up—strong, well attended, good minister, good sermons, a great choir, Tiffany windows, Bible classes afterwards. I liked this church. So I got involved in that a little bit, and then ended up getting promoted out of Dayton to Cincinnati at the end of the year.

I suppose I could have commuted from Dayton if I'd wanted to, but I'd always heard such great things about Cincinnati. And I ended up loving the city, but I didn't have the friendships that I'd had in the LTC office in Dayton. It wasn't long before I went looking around for a church; that definitely was playing a greater role in my life. I had asked for suggestions from the Dayton church, and they sent me to a couple that were disappointing in a way—older congregations.

So I remember looking at the paper one Saturday morning for different church services in the area. I saw a Methodist service that was real close, so I went there for what was advertised as a ten o'clock Bible study and an eleven o'clock worship service. I went in the side door, and there was a large group of younger people, which floored me because every other congregation I had visited was pretty old. There were probably seventy people in the group, and I just sat myself down. I think it was unusual that I just walked in by myself, so the usher came up to me and said, "Excuse me, are you coming for the Methodist service?" And I said, "Yes." He said, "Well this is not the Methodist service. Let me take you to the Methodist minister."

So I didn't know what the other group was, but I ended up getting introduced to the Methodist minister, and he seemed glad to see me. He said, "Why don't you sit down? Our worship starts at eleven and you can just read a magazine until then. We'll be glad to have you." Instead of reading the magazine, I went back to check out this other group and do something with my time. And for the first time I heard the Bible being explained in terms that I could relate to. There were a lot of friendly people there too, and I thought, This is very exciting; this church is kind of what I want. And so I sat through the service, and the Bible was really explained and used in the sermon in a way that I had never heard in the past.

I remember that my old Sunday school classes were disappointing because they would talk about the historical travels of Paul or something like that. But they never said, "These are the issues that you're dealing with as a young person. Let's look at the Bible to see God's perspective." The Bible was not a living thing in Sunday school; it was never used in a way that applied to my life.

I had gone through confirmation class when I was thirteen, but it was a joke. I remember being asked some questions for the council's assessment of whether or not I was ready to enter the church. I didn't know the answers to any one of them and still ended up being admitted to the church. It just wasn't real. God was pretty much whatever you wanted Him to be. There was nothing personal to Him; no character; no "This is right and this is wrong, and this is the reason why."

I'd kind of sell myself on different issues based on my own thoughts. Abortion—what's right, what's wrong? Who's to say? It's pretty much up to you. Sleeping with a girl? If you really love her, who's to say that's necessarily wrong? I was raised with a pretty strong conscience and moral standard, and yet it was never explained where that morality came from. It was just, "That's the way we are; it is a good code to follow; good people do this."

Gradually, as I got away from my family more and more, that code started to unravel and I questioned why I behaved in certain ways. Who's to say that drugs or sexual permissiveness are wrong? I still drew the line, but I could see that the line was moving.

So I started going to that church, and they invited me to go to a Bible study during the week, and I loved that. Again the Bible was really starting to talk to me. They also asked me if I wanted to join small study groups, and I certainly did. That was real valuable because I started understanding God in a more personal way. I understood what is expected of me as a Christian and why I need to know the Bible. I started learning about sin and about God's plan of salvation.

In spite of all my years at church, I had never heard anyone really talking about sin. It was always something the "fundamentalists" talked about; it was as if we were above that kind of thing. But it's embarrassing when you're in an individual study and they say, "We're going to talk about sin. What do you think sin is?" And I couldn't answer them. I said, "I know it's bad."

Anyway, I started studying more and more and really decided that you just aren't born Christian, as I was raised to believe. You need to know what Christ did and why he did it. You need to make some decisions about whether you accept Christ as savior and what that means in your life if you do. That definitely is how God planned it to be. As a little baby, you're not just born into this. You can't make those decisions. Even as a thirteen-year-old being confirmed in the church, I wonder if I was able to make life-changing decisions that I'd never drop or back away from.

I definitely see a series of events in my life as leading up to that decision to be a Christian and to really understand what that meant intellectually. Being a Christian wasn't this fluffy feeling anymore, just when I felt close to God. Happiness could be something that I experienced much more constantly than just those glorious moments of achievement. And it wasn't necessarily true for me anymore that being successful at LTC was being successful in life.

In October, a month after I became a Christian, LTC announced the closing of my regional office in Cincinnati. Everyone would be moved out of the region to other locations by the end of December, although a few people would move over to a small Cincinnati branch office. And that was a disappointment. Here I'd found a group of friends and had started a Christian way of life that I'd committed to as the most important thing to me. And all of a sudden—wow, bam, LTC says, "Mike, you've got to move."

There were some career opportunities that made moving more attractive than ever before. LTC was saying, "You can move into another region and finish another year of training to become a manager, or you can possibly step into management sooner by moving." Becoming a manager at LTC was attractive, definitely something that I'd set my sights on. I got excited thinking about that prospect.

As the December deadline grew closer and closer, they started moving me around to interview in different cities where I'd be considered for management. At first I tried to think through the possibility of whether or not a new city would have as good a church as the one in Cincinnati. But now I can see that when things start to happen, then they really begin to affect me emotionally. And as I traveled more and more, the emotional aspect became much more real to me. I flew out to Tulsa, Oklahoma, and it really hit home that I'd be leaving the people that I had grown so attached to and who had helped me so much on the spiritual level. Suddenly the most important issue in my life was whether or not I would find people to nurture my new spiritual life. Would it be replanted or would it wither in another location?

More and more I just didn't know what to do. I really prayed a lot to God to direct me and to tell me where He wanted me to go. I was really at a loss. This was one of the most difficult decisions I ever had to make. People from my church assured me that God would direct me—I just needed to have that faith. So I just clung to that, but we were in the second, third week of December now and things were getting heated. The managers were leaving at the end of December, and I was going off on Christmas vacation. I'd already gone through some final stages of interviews. Miami, New York, Chicago, and South Bend were all possibilities.

So on the last weekend I just walked around town on Friday night, really wondering what to do. I'd told my church friends that New York, Miami, and Cincinnati were my final alternatives. But the job offers in New York and Miami were so attractive that, really, in my mind, I had kind of eliminated Cincinnati. But I wasn't anxious to tell my friends that.

I remember looking in my journal later that Friday night. It has some of my thoughts from other significant moments in my life. I read through it, looking at what makes me tick. And I had analyzed myself before and really had seen that pride was the thing that drove me—being satisfied with what I was doing. It wasn't money; it was the esteem that came with accomplishments that turned me on. And from a Christian perspective that's interesting, because you read in the Bible that God opposes pride, that pride can be a hindrance to being open to the way God wants you to be. I ended up having a very meditative time that Friday.

And then Saturday morning I read the Bible in the morning. I was reading the Gospel of Matthew and I ran into a verse, Matthew 19:29, that says, "Whoever leaves their father, mother, sister, brother, children, or fields for my sake shall receive many times more and inherit eternal life." And that hit me like a brick. Up to now, LTC's stance was, "Mike, we only have so many branch positions in Cincinnati. Those are really for people from the regional office who have families and just aren't able to move to other cities. You are single. We see you as very movable, so you need to be considering somewhere outside of Cincinnati."

In my mind, staying in Cincinnati meant leaving LTC; but in the Scripture, it meant leaving my fields. From all of my intense prayers asking God to show me what He wanted me to do, this answer was the big one. I remember sitting in a chair and just sobbing, thinking that I was going to have to give up my fields, that God was calling me to do that. And yet, at the same time, I knew it was right because my spiritual life had become the most important thing in my life. Sure, I might be able to go into some of those cities and maybe they'd have a respectable church, but who's to say that I'd have the kind of relationships that had helped me here? How long would they take to develop? Would I be moved by LTC again just when I started establishing them? I had no way of knowing.

At that moment I was really letting go of the big security in my life—LTC. I really see God working in that decision to challenge my security and to force the issue.

The next day I called my parents and told them I had decided to leave LTC. My dad's reaction was, "This is a real mistake. I can't believe you're making that decision." My mom was more supportive in saying, "I know you've thought a lot about it. And whatever you decide, we'll support."

So on Monday morning I had to face my manager, who had gone through so much in sending me to so many places. I had already told him how important my church was to me. But he had said, "Well, I'd like to pursue this anyway and have you check the churches in other cities, and you can determine if it's right when the job offer comes in." So as I was preparing for work that morning, I thought, You know, Mike, it's not necessarily true that you have to go in and tell LTC that you've decided to leave. Why don't you go in and just tell them you've decided to stay in Cincinnati. Let *them* make the decision that you have to leave the company. I decided that was good strategy.

So that's what I did, and my manager couldn't believe it; that was the last thing he wanted to hear. He said, "I think you're making a serious mistake. They really do want you in these other positions. This is a chance for you to get into management. The door is open now, Mike. In the coming years I think there's going to be some consolidations, and I don't think the door will be open again." He really put on a hard press there. And I just said, "No."

I remember a lot of silent moments—he was a very wise manager and had a lot of good advice—and yet he just couldn't relate to that decision. So then he said, "How about if you commuted to Dayton?" And I said, "No, I'm not open to that." So he said, "Well, let me work on it." He ended up developing a scenario in which I would commute to Dayton, and he offered me a lot of juicy incentives to do that. I said, "No, I can't. The reason I'm staying in Cincinnati is because of what I'm doing after hours, and if I commuted I'd be taking away from that time. I might as well move if I'm going to do that."

He was very disappointed and finally said, "Mike, we've offered you so many different possibilities. You've gone at great expense to all these cities, and the one option we can't offer you insist on having. I don't see that there's a solution here. Are you prepared to leave LTC?" And I said, "Yes." That took him aback; he didn't expect that. He said, "I'll have to talk to the Cincinnati branch manager. I know they've absorbed a lot of people in the branch, but I'll ask him what he can do. If he refuses, then I'll have to go to the regional manager, his boss, and force you in."

So that didn't sound great, going to a place where they really didn't want me. But I said, "Well, so be it." And it did take the regional manager to force me into the branch.

So I went on vacation and came back to the branch in January—not really knowing what was going on. One of the managers called me and said, "Mike, we have an opportunity for you to consider. I think it's the right one for you." They were looking for people with a systems engineering background and with some marketing flair to help give seminars in the marketing center.

This was a new concept for LTC—asking prospects to come into LTC for seminars so that we could sift through them there and pass the good leads to the marketing reps. There were some career and financial risks there for me, but it sounded like an opportunity, and it was different from what I was doing before. So I took the position, and it was golden. I made much more money than I ever did before.

With the way everything worked out, I definitely see God forcing me to take a leap of faith, and yet being there to support me when I came out of it. It increased my faith a lot to see again that there is a living God and that He really does bless acts of faith. In fact, He encourages them; He demands them. This isn't just some philosophy that's nice to do.

So I continued the new job, and, with the church, I continued to grow spiritually and to take on more responsibility in leading Bible talks and in meeting the spiritual needs of other people who wanted to follow a similar path. Also, this past year I got married. That was certainly a big decision, but it was an easy one just because it was so right. God made it clear in my heart that Kim was the one for me. She and I have the same focus; God is also the number one thing in her life. The Scriptures show how God expects marriages to work. When you both have a focus on Him and you're striving for the same thing, there's a unifying force there. You actually help each other to change because you're mutually striving for the same ideal. And there's a bond and a unity that you can't get any other way. That is how God expects Christian marriages to last; it has been very rewarding for me.

So, as time went on, I took on more church responsibilities after hours. I led a downtown Bible talk that meets during the noon hour for professionals, and I also led the one in the evening hour. This became very demanding, combined with my marriage and job. At that point I saw that either I stopped taking on additional church responsibilities or I left LTC.

Then, later in the year, the church came to me and asked me if I would consider going full-time as a church counselor, and I just knew my heart was there. At that time I think I still would have liked to have been a manager with LTC. It would have been fun, and I'd have learned a lot from going to LTC management schools, which are in a class of their own. But when the church first asked me to consider going full-time, I remember I had a grin from ear-to-ear. My heart was saying, "Mike, this is something that you've wanted to do. Man, you've *got* to do it." There's never been anything in my life so clear and sharp.

There's a story of me sitting in a restaurant with the guy who asked me, and we were looking at the menu. He said, "So, Mike, what do you think?" And I immediately said, "Oh, I'm just so excited about it." I was just grinning from ear-to-ear as I went on talking about the prospect of taking this job. But he was really asking about the menu. That's how excited I was about this job possibility.

There were some questions in my wife's mind about this change. She had already given up on her job as a research assistant to become a full-time counselor for the church. Certainly her security was changing if I decided to leave LTC, but she knew that it was right for me.

This was not a decision to simply take on the next level of responsibility in the church, either. It wasn't just a matter of becoming a counselor who taught small group classes during the week. This was a decision to eventually become a minister. And I had some questions about how big a stretch that would be for me. Could I do that? Could I have the spiritual insights to really call people higher and to make the Scriptures come alive for people?

One suggestion a friend made helped me a lot. He said, "Mike, look at where your life was two years ago and where it is today. And then extend that another two years or so and think where you'll be if you grow like you have in the past." That was helpful because I did see how I had grown in the past. And when I looked in the future, as farfetched as the idea of being a minister seemed to be, I did have a vision that helped me to say, "Yeah, I can do this."

Right now, I'm very satisfied with my decision to leave LTC;

I've had no regrets. I see that my life is really going toward something as never before. It's not the easiest life to lead, though. There's definitely a stretch for me emotionally, spiritually, and financially—and yet I've never been more sure about where I am. I just keep coming home to the idea that some day I'm going to account for my life to God. And in the end, there's really only one question that He's going to ask me about my life, and that is— "Did you live as a Christian or not?"

I think some people will say, "I hope so. Did I?" Or, "It seemed to me that I did." There'll be a lot of doubt. But *knowing* the Scriptures and *knowing* what God expects, I want to be someone who says, "God, I knew what it took. I knew the standard was high, and I know I fell short in some cases, but I know what Your promises are, too. And even though I'm not worthy of being with You, I know that You will accept me because of my heart and the decisions I've made—and because Christ is truly the Lord of my life."

In the end that's all that matters. This life just leads up to that.

In March and April my journey off the fast track took a turn that I never expected. But when I stopped working those long days at Procter & Gamble, I had the time and certainly the cause to question some long-held beliefs.

For many years I had thought that marriage and a high-paying, prestigious job were the two main ingredients for a happy life. Together they loomed on the horizon as an oasis in the desert. Marriage would ease my deep-seated loneliness; and the "right" job would not only bring financial security, but also a kind of personal security that I couldn't find within myself. I needed to know that I was valued by the world around me; I needed to feel that I had "proved myself."

At age twenty-eight, however, I had recently been divorced and had just walked away from my fast-track job at P&G—after I had invested two years and over $100,000 in tuition and lost income to get there. My oasis had turned out to be an illusion; the world had seemingly played a cruel trick on me. Or had I played one on myself?

In any case, I needed to discard my old map of the desert. But I did not have a new one to replace it. And that realization caused just as much anxiety and loss of sleep as had my job at P&G. This became another source of tension that I just could not seem to "work out" or "run off." As I look back, it's almost as funny to think about the exercise routine I adopted in Cincinnati. Every night after work I would drive over to a nearby high school football stadium and do a series of wind sprints. Back and forth across the dimly lit field I would run, arms and legs pumping, eyes straight ahead. I would dash for a hundred yards, rest for a moment, then turn around and start jogging the other way. "Okay, push it now, push yourself this time . . . Go!"

For about twenty minutes I would try to sweat out the day's frustrations; then I would pour myself into the car and go home. The shower felt so good. That was the best part—the feeling I had in the shower, that temporary feeling of satisfaction that comes after a hard workout. As time went on, though, it wore off quicker and quicker. Had I pushed myself hard enough? Had I done enough sprints? It seemed as if no amount of "back and forth" would ever sustain that feeling of inner satisfaction.

Finally, at some point during my "special assignment"—I do not remember exactly when—I began to think about channeling some of my energy in another direction. And, like Mike Sinclair, I guess I had an "openness" to exploring religion and spiritual issues. Even though I believed in the existence of God, some kind of God, I had done no further thinking or studying since Sunday school. But now, because I was not getting anywhere with my current approach, I decided to try another form of "exercise."

Really, that was about all there was to it. No sudden vision. No flash of insight. For some unknown reason, I decided that "spiritual exercise" might deserve the same discipline I applied to physical exercise. That was the depth of my thinking. I mean, I did not want to go through life with the spiritual equivalent of a pot belly.

In March I began a new regimen. I read from the New Testament every day, went to Mike Sinclair's weekly Bible study, attended Sunday services at different churches, and read a book entitled The Road Less Traveled *by Scott Peck.*

The pieces of my emerging spiritual life did not all fit together neatly, however, and I eventually drifted away from Mike Sinclair's Bible studies and his church. Nonetheless, fostered by my understand-

ing of The Road Less Traveled, *I began to develop the perspective that a Christian life is akin to a journey toward God—a God that is somehow within everyone, including myself. M. Scott Peck writes: "In my vision the collective unconscious is God; the conscious is man as individual; and the personal unconscious is the interface between them."*

That was a radically new idea for me. God is actually in me? Previously my concept of God was that of a distant, lofty figure who would simply give me a "thumbs up" or "thumbs down" signal after I died; God did not seem relevant to me now, today. And the fear of "going to Hell" in the distant future was not a good enough motivator for me to take religion seriously or, frankly, to reexamine my approach to anything. But when my whole model of Christianity began to change, when I started to believe that now, at every moment, God was somehow within me and I in God, I saw my own life in a new light.

I began to realize that the understanding of my skills, interests, and motivations—the self-knowledge gained in my career-counseling sessions—could be an essential part of my journey toward God. If, to the best I could determine, the God within me pointed toward a certain road, then I felt it would be wise to follow it—even if it led off the fast track, or toward a "road less traveled."

By viewing my departure from P&G and my decision to try writing as part of a journey toward God, and by putting the rest of my life in that new framework, I felt a lot less lonely. In fact, I was excited to think that I could be on a lifelong spiritual quest toward God and excited to think that I could use whatever happened to me along the road—"good" or "bad"—as raw material to further that journey.

Excited, but also scared. Scared because all of my excuses for feeling unhappy or unfulfilled were stripped away. I could no longer blame a person, a job, or anything else in the outside world. I had power within me to transform my life. And I was responsible for finding the right path to connect with that power—and for attaching meaning and purpose to everything in my life.

With regard to this new and awesome responsibility, I identified with what Scott Peck felt when, as a fifteen-year-old, he left the prestigious prep school he had attended for nearly three years:

If I returned to Exeter I would be returning to all that was safe, secure, right, proper, constructive, proven and known. Yet it was not me. In the depths of my being I knew it was not my path. But what was my path? If I did not return, all that lay ahead was unknown, undetermined, unsafe, insecure, unsanctified, unpredictable. Anyone who would take such a path must be mad. I was terrified. But then, at the moment of my greatest despair, from my unconscious came a voice that was not mine: "The only real security in life lies in relishing life's insecurity." Even if it meant being crazy and out of step with all that seemed holy . . . I had decided to be me . . . I had taken the leap into the unknown . . . I had taken destiny in my own hands.

And so had I. Finally.

QUESTIONS, QUOTATIONS, AND EXERCISES

GENERAL:

    a. What incidents, images, ideas, or words from this chapter stand out for you?

    b. When were you happy, sad, or mad as you read it?

    c. What advice would you like to have given Mike?

    d. What are the lessons for your life?

FOCUSED:

"At that moment I was really letting go of the big security in my life—LTC."

    a. How much security do you feel now? What are the main sources of this security?

    b. To what extent could reliance on any of the above be a limiting factor in your life?

    c. To what extent do you agree with M. Scott Peck's quotation from *The Road Less Traveled* that "the only real security in life lies in relishing life's insecurity"? Why or why not?

"At first I tried to think through the possibility of whether or not a new city would have as good a church as the one in Cincinnati. But now I can see that when things start to happen, then they really begin to affect me emotionally."

a. Think of three significant school, career, or life decisions. What did your head tell you? What did your heart say?

b. What are your head and heart telling you about your current place in life—or your next anticipated move? Are there any conflicts?

c. What can you do to creatively reconcile the differences?

"One suggestion a friend made helped me a lot. He said, 'Mike, look at where your life was two years ago and where it is today. And then extend that another two years or so and think where you'll be if you grow like you have in the past.'"

a. In the areas of life most significant to you, where were you two years ago compared to today?

b. What growth has taken place over the last two years? What has facilitated that growth? What barriers did you have to overcome? What did you have to let go of?

c. If you extend your growth two years into the future, what do you see for yourself? What can you do now to facilitate that growth?

Heading Home

IT HAD BEEN ALMOST A YEAR since I had backed a rental truck out of my parents' driveway in Wallingford, Connecticut, and headed for Cincinnati, fifteen hours away. I was off toward a new job—a new life, really—and this departure felt different from any other, more permanent.

Ten months later, though, I was coming back. My money was gone, and there was no publisher's advance in sight. The "prodigal son" was returning, jobless and broke. And even though my parents were extending their customary welcome, under the circumstances it could have been a long, lonely, and depressing ride home.

But it was not such a bad ride at all. I was not going home because I had to; I was going because, for the first time in my working life, there was something that I really wanted to do, something that aroused my passion. I felt that I was beginning a new adventure; and whatever lay ahead was part of a great and exciting mystery, a mystery that I was rushing to meet.

So my ride home was more like a flight. Neither money problems nor one writer's criticisms had stopped me from pursuing my book idea, my dream. On the day after Sarah Isaac's discouraging phone call, a friend had said, "You shouldn't give up because of this one voice. Maybe you just need to hear other voices."

My friend was right. Before I left Cincinnati, I "test marketed" the first three stories of this book with some other young adults. The results were encouraging. It seemed that the stories had provided the stimulation—as well as a convenient frame of reference—for the readers to reflect on their own educational and career choices. More than anything else, I think they liked knowing that they were not alone in their doubts about their careers. So I decided to keep moving forward, to do whatever it took to find a publisher and finish this book.

Moving home was only the first step. The second was calling up and asking Citibank and the Harvard Business School to grant me a deferral on several student loans. That was easier than I thought; they each gave me a six-month grace period. But then again, what could they say when I told them that I simply could not pay the $1,800 I owed next month?

Deferring my loan payments was nothing, however, compared to the next hurdle I faced. I had to convince someone in the book world that an unpublished author with a partial manuscript should be given an advance. It's hard enough to find an editor who will read your material, let alone buy it.

Fortunately I did know several people with connections to the publishing world, and I sent out a proposal to them. The response that trickled back was less than overwhelming. The idea of an oral history about the career choices of high achievers seemed to be appealing, but nobody thought that a simple collection of stories would sell. What was the point?

Finally, after a month of increasingly desperate phone calls and letters, I got my first break. Frank Silvers, a high-powered agent in New York City, said that he would read my proposal and give it serious consideration. Two days later I got on the train to New York and made a personal delivery of my manuscript. Then, after having devoted so much time to the selling rather than the writing of my book, I took a cab to a prearranged meeting place for another interview, this time with a Wall Street investment banker named Alison Kearny. Knowing that Frank Silvers wasn't going to report back for six to eight weeks, I was glad to spend a good portion of that agonizing period engrossed in her story.

When it comes to overcoming obstacles and "doing whatever it takes," Alison Kearny is the one who could write the book. In my situation I needed to hear that kind of story.

The Investment Banker: Alison Kearny

"It was one of those times where you just drag
yourself out of bed. You've had three hours' sleep,
and you've been doing this for weeks. You're
tired, but you've got to keep going. It was
simply like dying."—Alison Kearney

*A*T 6:45 P.M. ON A WEDNESDAY, I sat in a McDonald's on
*Fifth Avenue in Manhattan hoping that Alison Kearny would
keep our 7:00 appointment.*

*A friend on Wall Street had told me that Alison had a rare com-
bination of talent and humility, and that she had come a long way
since her $5.00-an-hour job as a secretary in an automobile repair
shop. That piqued my interest.*

*Just two days before, however, another potential Wall Street inter-
viewee had canceled a Sunday appointment at the last minute. "I
know this is bad form," he said, "but I've been in the office all day,
and I've still got a lot more to do to get ready for the week." Thinking
that Alison also worked for a prestigious investment bank, I worried
that our upcoming interview would meet a similar fate. After all,
this was the middle of the week.*

*At 6:55, however, I could see a tall, graceful woman in a blue suit
striding purposefully down the street. Right on time, I thought, she
must have things under control.*

*Over the next three hours, I learned a great deal more about Alison,
the second of four children, raised near Atlanta. Her parents divorced
when she was a small child, and her mother remarried a man who also*

had four children. In overcoming her lack of money and her disdain for high school, Alison got to where she is primarily through her own hard work and determination.

I also learned that it is a good thing I had not tried to meet with Alison two months earlier.

I was the type of person who didn't get into trouble as a kid because I was so busy doing things. Even though I didn't follow the fast track right away, I was always a driven person.

Since I looked older than I was, I started baby-sitting at a really early age. On a Saturday I would be so busy: I'd have somebody from one until four in the afternoon and then someone else from five until midnight. I'd just book 'em. When I was twelve, I paid for a trip to Europe to visit relatives with money I had saved.

It was just my nature to work hard, I think. I really don't know why. There were a few things I wanted to do, and it took money to do them. I have always been the practical type. But whenever I get involved in something, I overkill. I played the clarinet all the way through junior high school, and I was really serious about music—I was going to major in it. I also played the oboe, the saxophone, the cello, and one summer I learned how to play the French horn. I even learned how to repair musical instruments. I just throw myself into things.

But when I hit high school—it's sort of bad luck—we moved out to a fairly rural area outside of the Atlanta suburbs. I went to a school that had a lot of farm kids and some racial and drug problems. Only about ten percent of the students there were serious about academics, and most kids didn't even talk about going to college. I was the type who could have been serious, but I really didn't like the school environment at all. And the fact that my mom had recently married a man with four kids who weren't as good in school as the four on our side lowered the expectations of everybody. There was no push to excel because my parents couldn't afford to send eight kids to college and because they wanted to set standards that everybody could achieve.

This was unusual for my family because my grandmother went to Smith College and so did everybody else in her generation that I can think of. My mom also went to a good school, and she was working on her doctorate at the time I was in high school. So the educational drive was there in our family. But at the time we just weren't encouraged to go to the best schools that we could.

Also, I made the mistake of becoming best friends with my older sister's friends. Since they had graduated by my senior year, there was nothing at the school to keep me really interested. So in the middle of that year I decided to drop all of my courses except the two that I would need to graduate and to take a full-time secretarial job at an automobile repair shop.

Don't ask me how I got my mother to agree to that. I didn't even let her come near the place because the guys were dirty and greasy and the environment was just awful. I think she just had a lot of trust in me—I was the one she put in charge whenever she went away. She also had too many other problems to handle to keep the reins on me.

My family was starting to break up again; my parents were going through a divorce. That made for a lot of complicated choices as my senior year was ending. They would pay for me to go to a local junior college, but I really didn't want to stay at home and do that. And I considered going to Smith to keep up the family tradition—I applied there and got in. But I knew my grandmother would have to pay for it if I went, and I just had a lot of trouble with the idea of going to a very expensive school and wasting someone else's money when I had no idea what I really wanted to do there.

At this time my older sister, who was a year ahead of me, was going to the local junior college and living at home. She and I got together and decided to move out on our own. That would enable my mom to feel a little freer about getting a divorce because she would only have two kids to support at home. So my sister and I moved out, and we both did the same thing: worked as secretaries and went to school at night. And I tried to figure out what I wanted to do long term.

That was the first time I was on my own, and it was a meager existence, but we were happy. My sister and I got along really well. And I know it seems ridiculous, but I could support myself on my salary of $9,000 a year.

I also started to find something I really liked to do. After I had been on the job a short while, I started to teach myself how to do some bookkeeping things—like reconciling the checking account. After I had learned a little bit, the father of the guy I was dating—I had dated him since tenth grade—opened up an automotive shop. So I helped out on the weekends with those books. I was always on the go: working at my regular job for $5.00 an hour, going to school from six until nine at night, and working at the other shop on the weekends.

After a year of this, I started to look for a better paying job, and I found a medical clinic in downtown Atlanta that needed a secretary/administrative assistant type. I was seventeen or eighteen at the time, and everyone else who applied had formal training in accounting or at least more bookkeeping than I did. But I told the man who did the hiring that I was a good learner and that I would work hard. So he gave me the job on the premise that I would take an accounting course at night.

Well, this was like striking gold for me. I used to think that accounting was boring—it seemed dry and dull. But then when I found out I was good at it, that got me going. It was the type of thing that was logical, it made sense. You could figure it out down to the last penny and make it work. And it was the type of thing I could keep teaching myself.

As much as I kept learning, the business manager kept giving me more responsibility. I started doing the partnership tax return and all of their bookkeeping and getting involved with a lot of personnel and general management things. I was interviewing and screening all the administrative people for the clinic.

I liked my job because I got to see how a business functioned, and I thought I was the key cog in helping it grow. They seemed to need me. Every three months they gave me a raise; I went from $9,000 or $10,000 a year until I was making $13,000 when I left after two years. That seemed like a big accomplishment at the time.

What led you to keep taking classes?

Well, there was this expectation in my family that came from my grandmother—she is just the smartest woman I've ever known. I would have felt I was letting her down if I had just kept working and not gone to college. So I started at the local junior college because it was inexpensive and close to my job. When I moved to my new job it wasn't so convenient any more, and I also found out that some of the courses I was taking from the junior college wouldn't transfer to a four-year college. So I decided that I needed to transfer to a four-year college in Atlanta. At least I would be able to count my night courses there toward a bachelor's degree, which I guess I always knew I would get.

Going to school part-time, though, you never get the feeling of what college is really like. You're there at night so you've got older people there with different goals; and you've got teachers, who, I think, are a little more lax at night than they are during the day. It's not a fun environment—you do it because you think you have to.

Even so, I think what really made me want to go to school full-time occurred when I drove my younger sister (two years younger) out to the University of Southern California. My mom was in a better position financially with only two kids at home, so my sister went straight from high school to college. This was after I had been on my new job a few months—I still liked what I was doing—but I was putting in so many long hours between working and going to school.

When I took my sister to her dorm, I saw all these young people who looked like they were going to have a good time. They would get a good education, but still enjoy things and be able to lie out in the sun. They would just have a lot more free time and more fun than I was having. So I thought, "Well, if I can arrange the finances, this is something I would like to do."

One key thing I forgot to mention was one of the reasons my sister and I moved out on our own. We knew that if you could establish your independence from your parents for two years you could get financial aid without listing your parents' resources. So when I decided to go to school full-time, I was able to qualify for a lot of financial aid.

I guess there have been times when I've looked back and felt that I wasted two years. I've seen other people who got to places before I got my act together. But I learned a lot in those two years, and I also used them to get around the financing problems.

It's funny, if you look at my grades from the part-time school, I had mostly B's and C's until I took business courses. From then on I had straight A's. I'm not sure that I would have discovered my interests if I hadn't worked for those two years.

I also met a lot of people that I would have never known otherwise, typical blue-collar workers. They're very nice people; they just don't have much ambition. It was worthwhile to realize that I didn't want to live that type of existence. That gave me a little more drive when I hit school. I wasn't there just to goof off. I kept a 4.0 GPA the whole time I was in college. And I certainly wouldn't have done as well if I had gone straight from high school.

The guy I dated in high school had a strong enough background for college too, but he kept saying he couldn't afford it. I just thought, "You can do anything you want to if you just put your mind to it—just learn the rules and do what's necessary." But my friend still hasn't gone to school.

This may sound totally ridiculous, but there's a song from Pink Floyd's *The Dark Side of the Moon* album that was my theme song in high school. It's called "Time." And the words were sort of my driving force. This may seem cornball, but I'll read a bit:

> Ticking away the moments that make up a dull day,
> Fritter and waste the hours in an offhand way.
> Kicking around on a piece of ground in your hometown.
> Waiting for someone or something to show you the way.
> Tired of lying in the sunshine,
> Staying home to watch the rain,
> You are young and life is long
> And there is time to kill today.
> And then one day you find
> Ten years have got behind you,
> No one told you when to run,
> You missed the starting gun . . .

I think that song fits—it meant a lot to me. When I went away to school I thought, You know, I'm going to do something. I didn't want to be like some of my friends who were waiting for somebody or something. I did what I had to do, and the gap between me and my old friends has gotten wider and wider.

Anyway, I wound up going to a school on the West Coast that had a good business program. My first choice was Georgia Tech, but I didn't have strong enough grades to get in. So my plan was to transfer to Tech before my junior year. (I was a sophomore already because of the credits I had earned.) But even after getting a 4.0, Tech still didn't accept me. I was frustrated, but at that point I thought, "Well, I guess I'm here to stay."

When I started at college full-time, I had been used to working forty to forty-five hours per week, going to school two to three nights per week, and almost always working Saturdays. I had one or two nights and Sundays free. Usually I'd try to get some rest and do homework during those times. So when I hit college and saw how much free time I had, I couldn't believe it. I was ready to book three times as many classes as I needed. But I did want to use my free time to have some fun, too.

Although I was at a good school, it's pretty heavily into fraternities and sororities. The social nature of the school starts right there. And a lot of women there seemed more interested in finding a husband than anything else. But the school had a lot more to offer, and I got involved in all sorts of things. I was asked by the people in my dorm to run for dormitory president—somehow they thought I was capable of being president even though I hadn't really done anything. That meant a lot. Then in my second and third years I also became treasurer of the student body and was elected as an officer in tons of clubs. This was all on top of working twenty hours a week as a purchasing clerk and keeping a 4.0 in the honors program. I kept challenging myself. I knew I had a weakness in English—my writing skills weren't strong. So I was torn: do I take an honors English course and possibly kill my average? Well, I decided to take it. Then I worked my tail off and managed to get an A.

I guess I just like to learn. I always seem to find my weaknesses and then thrust myself into a situation where they are exposed, just to see how much I can do. So far I've done all right, but we'll take a look at more of that later.

Another issue for me was that I had to keep my grade point average up to retain my financial aid. And when I got that 4.0 in my first year, I sought out scholarships that people in the financial aid office didn't even know existed. I wrote every women's association and accounting association I could find. I can't remember who all gave me scholarships, but I know I was the first person to get a $2,500 scholarship from the American Accounting Association. Altogether I think I found over $4,000 on my own.

When I first went to college, my professional goal was to become a CPA and to be paid well. The accounting department was the god there. That's where the smartest students went. So I gravitated toward that, and I wound up getting the top scholar award given by the department. If finance had been the most prestigious department, I probably would have concentrated on that. The finance professors were all pulling for me to switch. As it was, I decided to double major in accounting and finance, and I did it by taking summer school courses between my junior and senior year.

I also got involved in what they call the Educational Investment Fund, which was about a million dollars that a group of thirteen students managed. It was real money—part of a two-semester finance course, usually for people in the MBA program; but I was able to get in. The first semester of my senior year I was the accountant for the fund, and I had to keep track of all the trades we did. That was where my interest in capital markets and finance really took off.

I spent so much time—I read the *Wall Street Journal* page by page every day—and I got so much out of the class. It broadened my whole understanding of business because a lot of accountants are only interested in the past history of a company. But in finance you're trying to decide whether to invest in something, so you've got to figure out how it will work in the future.

When I graduated, I had three times as many accounting courses as I did finance. So I didn't want to change gears as far as my short-term career thinking; I went ahead and passed the tests for the CPA. An investment career seemed like more of a long-term possibility, although I did apply to Stanford's MBA program. I didn't get in. They said I needed work experience. I was hoping my years before college would qualify, but I guess that wasn't professional enough.

So my plan was to work for a couple of years in public accounting and go back to school for an MBA to make the transition into investment work.

In the meantime, I had to figure out where I was going to work and what kind of accounting work I wanted to do. Most other people were trying to get an auditing job in Los Angeles. That was the big deal for accounting majors. So what did I do? I picked the hardest city to get a job—San Francisco. No companies recruited from there. And I picked the hardest area of accounting to get into—tax. Audit sounded boring, and I wanted to work out of an office, not a traveling bag. I knew that the tax field only hired people who had a master's degree in tax, but I somehow managed to get several offers from big accounting firms in San Francisco.

So I chose one firm that I liked and started off with ten other people who already had a technical education in tax. But I put my nose to the grindstone, and my boss—I still consider him my mentor—he and I just hit it off. He liked the fact that I worked hard and had a certain maturity compared to others who were just starting. You don't normally find a partner in charge of the tax practice in a five-hundred-person office paying attention to a new hire. But he was always doing little things to make me feel I was special. Pretty soon I was at the top of my group. I just worked hard at it, and I liked it a lot.

I also did things like volunteer to do current-events seminars. Most people at my level wouldn't do that because you have to get up in front of everybody and talk about what's going on. I would spend forty hours in preparation, mostly reading, before I got up to talk for fifteen minutes. I did it because I knew I would learn more by forcing myself to speak in front of people. I would also learn to get over being scared to death—and I did.

The tax business is seasonal, so my worst period was three weeks of working seventy to seventy-five hours. At the end of that I was just bonkers—I was so tired. The more typical week would be fifty hours. Not bad . . . manageable. But it's funny—when I worked in public accounting the big firms had the highest standards and drove you the hardest. I thought that I could never do this and have kids, that people who try and do it are crazy. But when I compare it to where I've been since, I think I could have done it then—had kids and raised a family successfully.

I have to keep asking myself, Do I want a career that is going to monopolize my life? But how do you decide when something is monopolizing your life?

I remember trying to figure out if you could do what was required in a big firm to become a parent and still have a family. It's hard because you have to work nine or ten years to be a partner. So a woman who starts at twenty-five could become a partner in her mid-thirties. Then she'll have some leverage. That's the key. Losing a partner is a big loss to a firm. As a partner she'll be able to set her own rules, and she'll be able to have a family and maintain her career. Partners also get a lot of respect and credibility from clients when they say something. But it's hard for women who want to be truly respected in a firm. When you know it's going to take ten years to get there, and you probably can't start a family until afterward, you sort of wonder.

So for the first year I loved what I was doing in public accounting. I liked the people I worked with, and I was learning a lot. But after that year I thought, Is this really what I want to do? In ten years do I want to be an expert on the Internal Revenue Code?

I had a friend who had worked on the college fund with me, and he became an analyst at Salomon [a large investment bank] on Wall Street. He was making a lot more money than I was, and his work sounded fascinating—the kind of investment-related work I wanted to do. So I thought, What the hell am I doing? There's no reason to stay here.

I applied for the MBA program at Stanford, Harvard, Wharton, and Chicago. It's hard to walk away from a good work environment, and I was doing well on the job, but when I was accepted at Wharton, I knew I wanted to go. The only problem was that they sent me a letter that said: "Your finances don't make it possible for you to attend our school at this point. You should wait a year."

I thought, "Oh no! I finally get into my first choice, and they tell me I can't afford to come.

At the time I was carrying my undergrad debt, and I had also gone on a spending spree with credit cards right after college. So I was $10,000 or $11,000 in debt a year away from going to business school—where I'd be $40,000 or more in debt. I thought, I don't care. Just mortgage the hell out of me. But they said their debt limit was $35,000, so I had a problem.

To make it work, I really had to scramble. The whole year before I went to business school I didn't buy anything, and put all of my money into paying off my credit cards. I was finally able to pay them off—my salary had gone from $21,000 to about $32,000. Then I asked my grandmother to guarantee that if there were a shortfall in the second year of $10,000, she would pay for it. And then I told her she would never have to pay it because I would get the scholarships necessary to cover the difference. And that's what I did, using the same method I used in college.

So after all of this, I was very nervous about business school because I knew it would be tough to be at the top of my class. You know it's competitive; you know there are a lot of good people. And I think I'm one of these people who don't have a strong self-image. It's almost like I've got to be the best at what I do because I thrive on my own accomplishments.

I really worked hard from the start, but one thing that was difficult was not getting any feedback on how you're doing for a long time. I'd always thrived on knowing that I was doing well. I had a competitive roommate the first semester who was very smart and who didn't have to work as hard as I did, so that made me even more nervous. I was also used to becoming a leader in whatever group I joined, but I didn't win any of the positions that I ran for at the business school. All of a sudden you feel you're run-of-the-mill. Fortunately I had one thing I could count on: accounting was a breeze. If that had been hard, I might have really been in a sweat. And once I realized that I was going to do okay in everything else, too, I was a lot more relaxed. But the first year was bad.

Even though her first year was "bad," Alison wound up graduating from business school with honors. And by then, she had an even more difficult challenge in mind.

Before business school, I had a very naive, rosy picture of what investment banking was like. I just thought it was an exciting, well-paid job that moved with the market. Each day you'd be able to say the market did this and I know why. Somehow I pictured the whole investment field as individuals with stocks. To me, the market was the place my grandmother had stocks and never knew what to do with them. That's really what I thought.

Then I found out early on in school that investment banking was the "in" thing to do, but I didn't know how I could differentiate myself from all of these other people who were going after it. And when I found out more about the lifestyle, I thought, Gee, this isn't what I really want. I want to have a good career, but I don't want to start something that I wouldn't want to be doing five years from now. So my strategy was to get a summer job in investment banking and see what it was like.

I tried. I interviewed and everything, but I didn't know enough about the field then. I thought I did, but I didn't realize that it's very hard to get a summer slot. And I made the mistake of not applying to the small investment banks for summer jobs until I realized that I wasn't going to get a job from one of the top twelve. By then it was too late, and I wound up working for a small consulting firm in Atlanta for the summer. It was fun, though, to be home and stay with Mom for the first time in many years.

It was also fun to see what a small consulting firm was like, and I did get to do an interesting project involving financial institutions. But I came back to business school thinking, All right, I'll go for investment banking and try to find something in my background that will give me a competitive advantage. There didn't seem to be many people at school who were specializing in financial institutions, so I decided to focus on that niche. I read everything I could find about it, and I decided that my background was best suited to mortgage finance, a growing area.

I was also looking at commercial banks because the lifestyle looked better there. And, at that time, I had become involved in a serious relationship with Alex, a business school graduate who worked for a corporation in New York City. I thought it might work out for the long term, so that just complicated things further. But I couldn't let that relationship influence me one way or the other because we weren't engaged. There was no commitment. If there had been a commitment, it's possible that I would have gone straight to commercial banking, even though I might have regretted not trying investment banking.

Anyway, I just agonized over the decision for a couple of months. I talked to the accounting department, and the guy who taught a course on career management, and Alex—poor Alex. I probably chewed his ear off.

So, during the recruiting season, I did well with investment banks this time. My final choice boiled down to becoming a specialist at a prestigious investment bank or becoming a generalist at an excellent commercial bank that didn't carry quite the prestige as the investment bank. Coming out of business school, you can get caught up in thinking that investment banks are a step up and commercial banks are a step down. And I'd been climbing the ladder a long time.

Then when I laid it all out on paper, the one thing that stood out was the potential to make a tremendous amount of money at the investment bank. The first-year salary was about $70,000 and bonuses were supposed to be $25,000. Second-year guaranteed salary was $90,000 plus the bonus—and they said people always make over that. I knew that two or three years down the road it would be $100,000, $200,000, or even $300,000. Even with living in New York, I knew my $40,000 debt would be gone in two or three years.

Then you look at the commercial banks with starting salaries of $55,000 or $60,000. In two years there was a gap between the two jobs of easily $50,000 to $100,000. That difference alone could wipe out my debt.

So there's the money, and it may have been an even greater disparity than I speculated. Then you say to yourself, "Well, I always wanted to work in investment banking. Everybody says it's an unbelievable lifestyle. But are they just being macho? Can I handle it? Isn't this the ultimate challenge? They only hire the cream of the crop, and I can be one of them."

It's hard to walk away from that when you can look at the commercial bank and realize that that's something you can still do after trying investment banking. You can't easily go from a commercial bank to an investment bank, but you can do it the other way around. Then I thought, If I go to the investment bank I might lose Alex in the process. If the hours are as bad as people say, I'm not sure he's going to stick it out.

What do I want out of life? Do I want to be by myself when I'm forty years old at an investment bank? Or do I want to have somebody to be my husband and to be the father of my kids? Am I even going to be able to have children if I go to an investment bank? And once I get there and make all that money, can I get out? Can I walk away in three years and take a four hundred percent pay cut and say that's okay?

It finally came down to the fact that even though I might lose Alex, he should be willing to stick it out for at least a year, maybe two, if he knows me well enough to know that I don't want that lifestyle long term. If he doesn't . . . that's just a risk I'll have to take because I can't walk away from investment banking without trying it. What if we break up for some other reason? I'll always regret not having done it. I sort of *had* to do it.

Even when I turned down the commercial bank, I told them I wasn't sure the investment bank was going to work. I was pretty candid in saying that I felt my lifestyle would be better with them, and they were receptive to those thoughts. On the other hand, I couldn't even ask the investment bank, "What are the hours like?" I was scared they would think I didn't want to work. Think about it—how can you ever go to work at a job and not know what kind of hours they expect from you? Why should that be a problem to ask? It's ridiculous.

What did you think the hours would be?

On weekdays I thought that you would probably work until seven o'clock and maybe one or two nights you would work till nine or ten. And I thought you would have at least two weekends off during the typical month.

I was in training for the first three months, and that fit my expectations. After you get over being scared, you realize that you don't have to do all of the stuff they give you and you can get out by seven o'clock. But by September I was out of training and put into a department. The first job I'm given is working for a guy who's a perfectionist—very smart and hell to work for. I learned a lot from him, but he ran me into the ground. And Alex went off the deep end the first weekend I had to work. Any time a crisis developed at work, he was in desperate need of attention. The whole thing was unbelievable.

During the last week of this assignment, there was a road show presentation, and things started to blow up as people began finding mistakes in our slides. I had killed myself—working until midnight every night including weekends. I was so worn out. It was one of those times where you just drag yourself out of bed. You've had three hours' sleep, and you've been doing this for weeks. You're tired, but you've got to keep going. It was simply like dying. I had circles under my eyes that just wouldn't go away. I wasn't eating—I lost five or six pounds in one week. But my adrenaline was so pumped I had no appetite whatsoever—I couldn't look at food, I was so wired. When things started blowing up on the last day, I would have just lost it if somebody had said the wrong thing. I would have just lost it.

Altogether, we went to seven cities in five days—helicopters between places. Some people would say it's exciting. But you're just trying not to say something dumb to the client, and you're so tired. And because you're responsible for the luncheon, your boss is picking on you to make sure that the food is on the table.

So that was my first assignment in investment banking. It turned out fine because we were able to fix the problems with the slides. And I learned a lot because we were talking about technical issues to investors, and I was one of three people in the bank who had to really go over the stuff. And there's Alex—giving me a hard time about not being able to spend time together. I'm thinking, It's just starting. I'm just starting. He's not even giving me a chance.

So then I think I went for a little while without dying, but it was only two or three weeks before it started again. That's the way this business works. You're given a transaction, and, especially when you're new, you're not given anybody below you, so you really have to do everything. They push so much responsibility on you. It is unbelievable. You find out that your body is capable of more than you thought. I never thought that I could proofread something and really focus on it at three o'clock in the morning after I've been working like that for a couple of days.

Slowly I began to put some weight back on. But I never did anything athletic; my apartment was a wreck; paying bills was a feat. I was a slave to the bank, and the rest of the time I spent trying to keep Alex happy. And he was much too demanding of me—because my job came first. It had to. It *had* to.

When you are starting a career in an area as demanding as this, that's when all the impressions are made. You've got to give it your all from the beginning. You can't say that you're going to leave at seven every day and establish a pattern so that people will get used to your schedule.

It's tough for somebody in a corporate environment to understand the pressure I felt. Alex worked long hours—ten or twelve hours a day—but his work schedule wasn't like mine. And the pressure at work was definitely worse than I thought it would be.

A typical week was eighty hours. You started between eight and nine and you would stay until nine or ten. If you left before seven it was rare, and most people order dinner at work. Very often you have to stay until midnight or later. And you almost always work one day of the weekend—maybe one and a half days, or occasionally both days when you are working on a project.

I even worked all night one time. At five o'clock one afternoon I was given something to proof by a guy who needed it for a presentation first thing in the morning. What made it worse was that I knew the guy had procrastinated before turning this thing over to me. But what choice do you have?

I became so wrapped up in work I didn't even care what the weather was like—I often didn't know what it was. Those days when we had bad snowstorms in New York City didn't faze me because I was getting out at three in the morning and there wasn't anybody on the road. But nobody thinks twice about the lifestyle; nobody bats an eye; it just goes on.

I never heard anybody at the firm talk about their family, about their wives or their kids. You get so caught up in the job and the deals you're working on—that becomes the center of your world.

Those other things are peripheral. But I didn't want to get caught up in an environment where Alex was unimportant. And nobody I worked with even knew he existed. There was rarely a social occasion where the firm invited spouses—which is just ridiculous. The Christmas party was not for spouses. The whole environment feeds on itself, and the bank is the center of the world.

My department was new, and that made it a little harder to manage, but the people at the top were out of touch with what was really going on. They should have known that I wasn't happy. And I didn't feel that there was a good forum to tell people how I felt. As a matter of fact, I tried not to tell people because I felt that you had to be a good little soldier during the first year.

Anyway, I did it—I kept up the pace for a few months. It was all work, work, work. And I was always so tired. On the weekends I'd want to sleep for twelve to fifteen hours. And when I'm tired, I look it. I get circles under my eyes—I just look like hell. All these other people keep plowing along with no sleep and they look fine —and I'm just dying. And every time something went wrong, Alex would have a fit. But you can understand where that is coming from. When something's bothering me and I call him at work and he tells me he's in a meeting, I go, "Aaaahhh . . . I have to talk to you now!" Can you imagine what it was like for him to call me at 10 P.M. at work just to say, "Let's talk," and to hear me say, "Oh Alex, I have so much to do." He'd say, "You can't even take ten minutes to talk to me?"

Well, his ten minutes were more like half an hour. But he hadn't talked to me or seen me for three days, so you can understand where he is coming from. At the same time, though, when you are in a situation where you are already suffering severely and some-body else keeps yanking your chain, you feel like saying, "Can't you just exist for a month or something?" But I didn't want to lose him either, and I knew he wasn't happy at all, even though he proposed to me in the midst of this whole thing, in November.

It doesn't sound as if you were very happy, either.

No, I wasn't. I was biting my nails off, and I was barely ever talking to my friends. Just so many things were being sacrificed. Whenever

I wanted to do anything important to me, it was so hard to get out of the firm for an evening, a day, a weekend. During the winter, I kept thinking I had to stay there for a year just because everybody says you have to stick it out for a year. That would have meant July.

But then, in February, my grandmother passed away, and I think that was a real turning point. I was in the middle of a transaction, and it was going to be a pricing week coming up. I had just killed myself over the weekend and had another week to go on this transaction, but that Sunday my mom called with the news, and I just took the week off. I was the key person on this transaction, but I said, "Sorry, I'm leaving." I felt guilty, but that's what you do; there's just no question about it.

So when I was home, I worked a little on the wedding and spent time with Mom. I just sat around and relaxed, too—something I hadn't been able to do for a long time. And I simply thought, There's more to life than working all the time. So I went back ready to do something about my situation. No one-year rule—that's stupid.

I pursued the commercial bank I had turned down earlier, and it took me three weeks to get through to the right people. When I did interview with them, my self-confidence was pretty weak. I was doing fine at the bank, but I didn't know it; they didn't tell me. So I wasn't sure I was going to get an offer, but they finally did come through, and I decided to make the switch. But I thought I should resign from my current job before I formally accepted the new offer.

So when I went to leave the investment bank they offered me a position in capital markets, which had hours of eight to eight. They said, "Look, you're at the top of our performance group." I said, "So how come nobody's ever told me?" But I was taken aback that they were willing to bend over backwards to keep me there. They threw tons of people at me to try and change my mind. It was hard; I had planned to just resign and walk away, but I took five days and thought about it.

People at the firm were saying, "Do it for six months. Give the new position a try. If you don't like it, we'll help you find a job somewhere else. And if the commercial bank's not there, we'll help you find another job." So I could easily say, "Well, why not do it for six months?"

But I finally did make the switch because I want something that is going to work if I have kids. I'm always going to have a career—I'll have a full-time nanny for the kids—and I don't want to do any job half-assed. A job that requires fifty hours a week, I think I can handle. A job that could require eighty—that would be cruel to your spouse and inhumane to your children.

So commercial banking can work. And over the next five years I'll bend a little toward Alex's career because of our plan for kids. Then I think he'll do the same for my career. We'll just have to be flexible.

So, after a few weeks on the new job now it's not quite as exciting, but I'm glad I made the switch. One thing that's funny is that I've seen a few people in short-sleeve shirts at the commercial bank. You would *never* see that in an investment bank. There you never see somebody who is overweight and doesn't look like the typical clean-cut bee-boppers who come from business school.

I think I'm getting off to a good start here, too; I'm doing what I did at the accounting firm. I'm starting to call up people I met during recruiting and ask them for lunch. That's one of the things you do when you're starting on a job to show that you care. I didn't do that at the investment bank. It was almost fated not to work out because I went in with the attitude, I'm just going to try this.

And Alex says I was a different person before, too. He had serious doubts about us, but now he says I'm back to the "old me." I think he's much more comfortable with the idea that I'm there if he needs me.

If I hadn't been involved with Alex, I probably would have stayed with the investment bank longer, but I think I still would have gotten out. It's hard to explain to other people, though. People at my new job have asked, "Why would you give up what you had for this?" A lot of them would give an eyetooth for an offer where I worked.

But now I'm just thinking, I did well at business school and at the investment bank, even though I didn't know it at the time. I think I'll also do well at my new job . . . and as a wife and mother.

By getting away from the investment bank for a week, Alison Kearny gained a fresh perspective on her career and the balance she wanted in her life. Shortly after I spoke with her, I was urged to make such reflection a regular part of my life.

"Every four or six months, get away for a weekend retreat just to think about what you're doing, where you're headed." That was one of several recommendations made by Bruce Bunker, minister of the First Congregational Church in Wallingford, Connecticut. To further my spiritual growth, he also counseled me to attend church weekly, to come in and talk with him (or another "spiritual director") on a regular basis, and to adopt a thirty-minute daily routine of reading, meditation, and prayer.

Since I had already begun doing some of those things and my outlook on life had changed as a result, Bruce's suggestions seemed right on the mark. Talking with him also reinforced my perspective on life as a journey toward God—a perpetual effort to grow in faith and to live more authentically. From our conversations, I started to grasp the significance of the Old Testament stories about the Jews wandering in the desert. No matter how great their sin, no matter how far they tried to separate themselves from God, He still kept searching for them. And I began to realize that even though I had been wandering in my own spiritual desert, God still cared for me, accepted me as I am, and was always waiting for me to turn in His direction.

In Surprised By Joy, *one of the books that Bruce recommended, C. S. Lewis writes of a trip to Oxford that holds symbolic significance for his own journey through life. Because I was in the midst of changing my direction, this passage made a deep and lasting impression:*

> *My first taste of Oxford was comical enough. I had made no arrangements about quarters and, having no more luggage than I could carry in my hand, I sallied out of the railway station on foot to find either a lodging house or a cheap hotel; all agog for "dreaming spires" and "last enchantments." My first disappointment at what I saw could be dealt with. Towns always show their worst face to the railway. But as I walked on and on*

I became more bewildered. Could this succession of mean shops really be Oxford? But I still went on, always expecting the next turn to reveal the beauties, and reflecting that it had been a much larger town than I had been led to suppose. Only when it became obvious that there was very little town ahead of me, that I was, in fact, getting to open country, did I turn around and look. There, behind me, far away, never more beautiful since, was the fabled cluster of spires and towers. I had come out of the station on the wrong side and been all this time walking into what was even then the mean and sprawling suburb of Botley. I did not see to what extent this little adventure was an allegory of my whole life.

QUESTIONS, QUOTATIONS, AND EXERCISES

GENERAL:

a. What incidents, images, ideas, or words from this chapter stand out for you?
b. When were you happy, sad, or mad as you read it?
c. What advice would you like to have given Alison?
d. What are the lessons for your life?

FOCUSED:

"I used to think that accounting was boring—it seemed dry and dull. But then when I found out I was good at it, that got me going."

a. What are you good at? Name three activities in which you feel particularly competent.
b. To what extent do these activities get you going? Why or why not?
c. What is holding you back? And what can you do about it?

"When I went away to school I thought, You know, I'm going to do something. I didn't want to be like some of my friends who were waiting for somebody or something."

a. Think of three periods of high achievement in your life. How would you describe your attitude then?

b. How would you describe your attitude over the last six months? How is that serving (or not serving) you now?

c. What kind of messages do you get from your friends? How do they serve you (or not)?

"I also did things like volunteer to do current-events seminars. . . . I did it because I knew I would learn more by forcing myself to speak in front of people. I would also learn to get over being scared to death—and I did."

a. How would you describe your current approach to learning? What are its strengths and limitations?

b. What subject area do you want to learn more about now? What skill do you want to develop? How will you start?

c. What one fear would you like to address now? How will you start? Who can help?

"I found out early on in school that investment banking was the 'in' thing to do."

a. What are the "in" things to do where you are now? What is your perspective on these things?

b. Think about three situations where you swam against the tide. How successful were you? What did it take to keep going?

c. How might you apply those lessons in your life now?

Pizza Man

FOR TWO MONTHS I had been awaiting the word from Frank Silvers as if he were a literary oracle rather than a literary agent. But when he finally called, his response reaffirmed my belief that the world doesn't offer many *yes* or *no* answers.

"Andy Fleming?"

"Yes—speaking."

"Frank Silvers, I've had a chance to look at your proposal, and I've done some light editing; overall, I think you write pretty well . . ."

(I'd heard that before.)

". . . And I think that this could probably be shaped into something pretty good . . ."

(Now *that* was good news.)

". . . But I really don't have the time to work on it—and this isn't the kind of book I normally handle, anyway. So I'll enclose a few thoughts when I return your proposal."

"Can you recommend someone else?"

"Yes, I can. Denise Stewart. I would just pick up the phone and call her."

I was excited and relieved that Silvers seemed to have taken my proposal seriously. My greatest nightmare was that some respected agent or editor was going to ridicule my work and expose me as the fool I sometimes thought I was.

So I did pick up the phone and call Denise Stewart, and she sounded interested as I outlined my idea. Then, after I received Silvers' comments in the mail, I worked feverishly for a week to clean up my manuscript and to clarify the concept of this book.

What I finally sent Denise Stewart was a proposal for a book that would contain a number of interviews as well as an overall conclusion that tied things together. I really didn't know what I would say, but I figured I would think of something after I had done all of the interviews.

While waiting to hear from Denise Stewart, I once again had one immediate problem—money. I needed a part-time, temporary job to fuel some more interviewing and writing; I had been running on fumes for the last month. After a brief search, I discovered that the best-paying part-time jobs were at United Parcel Service and Domino's Pizza.

Have I no shame? Could I actually go from HBS to UPS? Or could I put on a striped shirt and hat and start delivering pizza to people I might know here in town? I could just picture it—"Here's your fresh, hot Domino's pizza! Let's see . . . you ordered the mushroom and bacon, right?"

"Andy! What are you doing delivering pizza? You went to Harvard Business School—"

I would mumble something about being a struggling writer and reach out for a tip . . .

Regardless of the potential for such embarrassing moments, Domino's seemed to be the best option if I wanted to keep writing this book. So I went down to the nearest outlet, picked up an application, and started filling it out at the kitchen table when my dad came into the room. He had that furrowed brow—that look of disapproval—on his face. After all, he knew people in town too . . .

"You might want to hold off on that for a minute," he said. "Your mother and I have been talking about your situation, and I guess it comes down to whether or not we believe in what you're doing with this book. Well, we do believe in it; and we would like to loan you some money. Maybe this will buy you another month so you can keep interviewing and writing on a full-time basis."

A day later, MasterCard—still under the impression that I worked for Procter & Gamble—sent me a letter saying that they were raising my credit limit by another $1,500. That would also buy some extra time. I didn't know what my completed book would look like, but my chances of having a finished product seemed a little better.

I was also glad that I could put all of my time and energy into writing up my latest interview. This one was particularly absorbing because, of all the people I had interviewed, I identified most closely with a corporate lawyer named Matthew Goldberg. For two weeks Matthew's dreams were my dreams, and his dilemmas were my dilemmas. For two weeks his bouts of frustration and anger were mine as well. Those were two tough weeks.

The Corporate Lawyer: Matthew Goldberg

"That was when the sleepless nights started.
I used to lie there and think about how the end
was drawing near, how I was going to spend seventy
hours a week, doing what I knew I didn't want to
do. I'd sooner have shaved my head and
joined a monastery."—Matthew Goldberg

*I HAD NO TROUBLE finding the new Goldberg residence—
home of Matthew, a corporate lawyer, and Jan, a securities
analyst—even though it was tucked away in a heavily wooded development outside of Boston. Matthew's directions had been perfect.*

*"You'll see a golf course on your left about three-eighths of a mile
after you turn off the highway. Take a sharp right there onto Country
Club Road. Then follow that road for one and a quarter miles, passing the tennis courts and swimming pool."*

*It's not surprising that Matthew had given me such pinpoint
directions. After our conversation had barely begun, I decided that
this eldest son of a Boston College professor and a state senator from
Massachusetts, this graduate of Harvard College and Harvard Law
School, was one of the most thoughtful and articulate people I'd met.
And even though he was fully aware of his intellectual gifts, there
wasn't a shred of arrogance in his manner.*

*What did manifest itself at times, however, was a certain sadness—
a resignation, perhaps—that he wasn't combining his talents and interests in a way that was personally satisfying. Somehow, they had gotten lost along his career path.*

And speaking of getting lost: when I tried to get back to the highway after the interview was over, I found that my step-by-step directions were useless in the dark. All of the familiar landmarks—the golf course, the swimming pool—had disappeared.

Getting off Country Club Road can be much harder than getting on.

I was the kind of kid no one wanted in their Cub Scout den. I had a real reputation—which was deserved, unfortunately—for refusing to acknowledge authority. Thank God it's been modified over time or I might be in jail now. Even to this day, I don't like being told what to do or when to do it. I think I would be a terrible soldier if I were in the Army.

I can remember a Little League game one night; we had eight guys show up for the game, and I was the ninth guy. But I was shooting baskets on a court next to the field when the game was supposed to start. The manager's son came over and said, "What are you doing? You gotta play!" And I said, "No, I'm just not going to play; I don't feel like it." The angrier he and his father got, the more determined I became that I wasn't going to play. Naturally, I got thrown off the team. What a distinction—to be thrown off a Little League team. Unfortunately that's part of my history. For a long time I think I was something of a disappointment to my parents because I just didn't do well in school. I would hear comments like, "I understand so and so is doing very well. Why aren't you?"

I think the turning point for me was my freshman year of high school, when my father got to spend one year teaching in England. That meant that my sister and I were exposed to the rigor of the English grammar school. I started to do very well there mainly because the teachers didn't give me a choice—they were much stricter—and also because I felt the burden of being the only American there. I think that some of the British feel superior to us intellectually, and I remember thinking that I wanted to show them that that wasn't true.

So that was the year I started to believe that I would do very well. And when I came back from England, I wanted to show all those people who thought I was a clown that I could be one of the top students.

The other thing that happened then was that I became convinced —it was like an act of religious faith—that I had to go to Harvard, Yale, or Princeton. I felt that not going to one of those schools would really let my parents down. So that became a big obsession to me, although it was something that I never really examined. Never. I just believed—the way some people believe in God—that I was going to Yale or Harvard. And I was going to make sure that it happened.

So when I entered high school, I really was a different person. I was very serious about my studies, and, with some exceptions—I would slip here or there just because when you're fifteen or sixteen you can still get off the track—I worked real hard to get the best grades I could.

When I did start getting "A's" at school, it was great—I got a lot of positive feedback from my parents. It's funny: I really enjoyed pleasing them, but on the other hand it sort of created an expectation. That's what I perceived, anyway. In the few instances where I screwed up for one reason or another, I felt like they showed an unwarranted, disproportionate disappointment.

In addition to enjoying the pats on the head, though, I also started to find that a lot of stuff in school really interested me. Reading and discussing books for English classes, trying to understand what an author means, and realizing that a story can mean different things on different levels—that was all tremendously intriguing to me. My father and mother both read a lot, and my grandfather was a Talmudic scholar, so I think I inherited that scholarly trait. I found that with history and literature courses particularly, I was intrinsically interested.

I remember that it was really enjoyable to study about America's foreign policy and our involvement in World War I. I actually developed a set of convictions, real beliefs, that set me apart in class. I always took a strong position in class discussions, and I think that might be a little out of the ordinary for a kid to feel something so strongly in class.

The same thing held in English classes. I can think of actually being affected, physically affected, by books such as *Crime and Punishment*. There's a dream in that book about a man beating a horse that's so vividly described. The horse finally collapses under his cruel beating, bleeding and starting to throw up. It left such an impression on me.

Other things moved me, too. It seems like every English class read the same two plays, *Hamlet* and *Macbeth*. But I can remember reading passages in those plays over and over again just because the pure sound was so beautiful, the way the words went together. The fact that I was receptive to this sort of thing made me recognize that I had a sensitive, intellectual streak. I perceived that this was a rare thing, that this could separate me from other people. So I felt I had to hide that side of me in front of other people.

There's a line in a Billy Joel song—"Better not be a straight-A student"—because people will think that you think too much. When I was sixteen and seventeen, the ideal thing among my circle of friends was to do very well without apparently putting in a great deal of effort. Certainly you wouldn't want it known that you were interested enough to go off and read extra stuff. I had to be a little careful about letting things out in the classroom that would undermine my reputation as a bruiser on the basketball court. So I adopted this jock persona of someone who "played the game" well enough so adults would be happy with him—but certainly not someone who was going to shut himself in a room and open up Chaucer. That would be a damning piece of information.

As far as the college application process, I sat down with my father and mother, and we talked about applying to Harvard, Yale, and Princeton, and we threw in a couple of small places—Swarthmore, Haverford—but everyone knew I wasn't going there. My father wanted to make sure that all of the application stuff was done right, so I would write my essays, and he would pick them apart. Then he would hire his secretary from school to come to the house and type up a draft. Then we would go through that process again and again.

This was a very serious process—a real pain-in-the-ass process—trying to hone these things, trying to psych out the respective admissions directors by giving them everything they wanted, all that kind of crap. But I'm sure I had some pretty good applications compared to most people, mainly because my father took such pain to make sure they'd be that way.

So my final decision about college was really a prestige thing. I was primarily interested in Harvard or Yale just because the names were so magical. Also, I had a relative who graduated from Harvard in 1960, then went to Harvard Law School, and later made a pile of money on the West Coast. Everyone in the family thought he was really a hotshot.

So that was one of the things that sort of pushed me toward Harvard. I could get an elite degree, have a chance to play basketball, and be pretty close to home. Certainly I never analyzed the decision in terms of which college had the better history department, or something like that.

That was just a very pleasant time for me. When I think back to when I've been the happiest, I think about my senior year of high school as one of the highest points. I was doing very well academically, and I got into all these schools. People thought I was a very good athlete—I got a lot of respect for that—and my father had just bought a red Camaro for me to drive, and that made a hell of a big difference to people in high school. It just seemed that a lot of things had come together, and I felt blessed. I really did.

A big part of that feeling was, How can I really go wrong? If I don't go to Harvard, I'm still going to Yale. If I don't go to Yale, I'm still going to Harvard.

In the back of my mind, though, I did have some doubt about myself, as I'm sure nearly everyone does. It's the big fish in the small pond syndrome. It's one thing to get straight A's in high school, and I knew what it took to do that. But Harvard College was another thing.

To be honest, though, getting A's once I got to Harvard didn't seem much different from my public high school. You certainly develop better work habits there than you had in high school; and you read more books and undergo the discipline of writing long papers. Those are all things that have been helpful later on. But the most valuable part of Harvard—where the real maturation process happened for me—was not in the classroom, but in the dining halls.

I was lucky to hook up with a group of people that liked to debate things, mostly political things. What should the U.S. do vis-à-vis the Soviet Union? What's the best way to stimulate the economy? What should we do about the American hostages in Iran? It's funny, I don't think of these sorts of things now, but at the time they seemed so important to me.

And there was one history professor, Arthur Sullivan, who made a profound impression on my thought process. He was always asking you to critically examine the alternatives for any given situation. For example, "Is it fair to criticize the United States for intervening in Vietnam if the alternative is to let a hostile power achieve its goals?"

That kind of approach to problem-solving really made a big impact on me. I didn't go to Harvard because I felt like I had to learn how to think critically, but between my friends in the dining hall and Professor Sullivan, that's what happened there. And it was the most important thing that happened.

But one thing that didn't happen, to my regret, was that I never —not once in the four years—turned that kind of critical thinking toward my own career plans. I mentioned the relative who went to Harvard College and Harvard Law School—I had always heard that he was sensational—so early on at college I felt I knew exactly what I was going to do: I would go to Harvard Law School and follow in his footsteps. That was the same kind of thinking I had in high school; I simply focused on the next step in the process of "getting ahead."

At Harvard I was the kind of person referred to as the "grim pre-professional." Yeah, I wanted to go to Harvard Law School, and I knew it would take a hell of a lot of A's and an LSAT number in the 700's to get there. Upperclassmen would say, "Jack got a 796 on the LSAT, and he's going to Yale; Jill got a 770, and she's going to Harvard; but Harry, I don't know what the hell happened to him—he's going to the University of Virginia."

I didn't know what happened to these people after they got into law school or after they graduated. All I knew was that some were going to the place I wanted to go, and some were going to places I didn't want to go.

I look back on it, the whole thing was kind of funny. Had I turned this newly developed critical faculty toward the question of why I wanted to go to Harvard Law School so badly, I might have asked: "Where's it going to take me? What is practicing law *really* like?" The benefit of not asking those questions, however, was that I had a goal that kept me working like a dog. But, as I say, for some reason I never really thought about whether the goal itself was worthwhile.

That seems to be the way it is with a lot of people, myself included.

Yeah, and I think that if you want to be someone who makes a lasting contribution, someone who is remembered, you have to be the kind of person who knows what it is you really want. And you have to pursue that thing with passion.

Look at a guy like Larry Bird. From what little I've seen of him in personal interviews, he strikes me as just your basic, ordinary, beer-drinking kind of guy. But there's one exception, basketball, and in that one exception, he's a genius. I think "genius" is the appropriate word.

Maybe his genius comes from such an intense determination for basketball that long after everyone else has stopped practicing, he's still doing something a hundred and fifty times over that doesn't seem like a lot of fun. He's dribbling with his left hand or practicing a particular move. It gets dark and he's still doing it; he goes to sleep and he's still thinking about it; and he wakes up and goes to work on it again.

You think to yourself, Gee, I would like to have a passion like Larry Bird. I wish there were something I could be a genius in. But maybe it's a circular thing. I haven't found anything like that because I haven't pursued anything the way he does.

But you didn't spend time thinking about any career-related passions while you were in college.

That's true. I went through college learning from people in dining halls and trying to understand new issues by examining their premises. But I never applied that same rigor to my own career thinking. That was a separate compartment. I sure as hell wouldn't accept that lack of rigor in deciding who was responsible for World War I, but for some reason I accepted it for myself.

And let's face it: there is no thought required to go from Harvard College to Harvard Law School. In fact, it's easy: you don't have to ask yourself the hard questions. You can get the usual round of applause and pats on the head for moving the next step up the ladder.

And that approach had real benefits in my senior year, too. Compared to so many of my classmates who were going through extreme anxiety about their futures, I felt a little superior. There sure wasn't a question as to what I was going to do, even though my conception of what a lawyer did—to the extent I had one—was so vague. I thought of them as people who had to be articulate, who had to be persuasive, and I thought my strengths fit pretty well. I had this idea that being in a law firm would be a natural extension of being at college. I would do my work, hand it in, and take my pat on the head. People would recognize that I was doing good work, and we would all make up kind of an intelligent fraternity.

I can remember as a sophomore and junior in college, my dad and I would go to lunch with one of his former students. He worked at a major New York law firm, and I would go up to his office on the fifty-ninth floor of the General Motors building. The whole thing seemed unbelievable to me. The walls had expensive-looking artwork, and we would go to a club for lunch where everybody knew him by name. My head was swimming. I had no idea what he did during the day, but it sure looked good from the outside. It seemed like a natural extension of the path I was on.

And one summer I went to work for my hotshot relative on the West Coast. The guy was making a pile, and he had his own mansion—these things made an impression on me. I guess this could sound grossly materialistic, but I'm giving you my honest reaction. I didn't really tune in to what was going on around me on a day-to-day basis because for me, at the time, the end game was getting into Harvard Law School and getting my ticket punched. The destination—where that ticket would take me—I just accepted that as some place I would want to go. I didn't sit down with any lawyer and say, "You know, I'm thinking very seriously about doing this. Now what the hell is it that you do? What do you like and what don't you like about your work?" To the extent I did ask questions, they were along the lines of, "How can I facilitate getting to a place like this?"

My parents kept telling me that I had more in me than either of the two successful lawyers I'd met, and that strengthened the premise that I would follow in their footsteps. That's funny—it was an unfair mental process. I would allow evidence and data to collect that would strengthen the premise, but I never permitted anything to enter my mind that might weaken it.

But I'm not really sure you can ever get anywhere in life if you're always questioning what you're doing. I don't think Larry Bird becomes Larry Bird by saying, "Geez, does it really make sense for me to shoot five thousand hook shots every day? Is that really sensible? I have a certain amount of time to enjoy life—why shouldn't I have a Coca Cola with a friend?" As soon as you allow questions to creep in, you can undermine your determination. The next thing you know, you're not shooting the hook shot and then you're not playing for the Celtics. I believe that's inevitable if you ask too many questions, and I sure wasn't going to let that happen with Harvard Law School.

So when I applied to law schools, there was the same cast of characters—my dad, his secretary, and me—working on those applications. And if I wrote and rewrote my college applications five or six times, which feels like building the pyramids to a seventeen-year-old, I must have gone over them thirty times for law school. I applied to many of the same universities, and I thought even less about the differences between the schools than I had before.

As before, the admissions process went very well, and I was off to Harvard Law School. And again, maybe even more than before, I was thinking, Geez, this time around I'm *really* in over my head. That wasn't exactly true, but the truth of the matter was that I didn't do as well as I did at Harvard College. You just can't because you're going up the pyramid, and the competition is getting more and more intense. Now you're talking about a class of people who are unlike the diverse group you're with in college.

In college the admissions people are interested in knowing if you play the violin, or if you can run fast, or if you fit one hundred other criteria. In law school they care about two things: your GPA and your LSAT. So that doesn't make it the most diverse or interesting group of people, but it sure as hell makes it a very smart and determined group.

The big difference between a college class and a law school class is that in college you really are a spectator; but in a law school you can get called on at any time. The law professors use the Socratic method—asking you one question after another—and that created tremendous anxiety in me. I was very nervous about getting called on, especially the first few weeks. I'm sure everyone did this, but I would listen to every question and answer and then compare the answer given to how I would have answered. So often I thought, Geez, I don't think I could have done as well. Or, I just wouldn't have known how to proceed.

It's funny, though, when you finally have the experience, and you're called on by a professor who's good, he can get you to where he wants the conversation to go even if you're not sure of the facts or what the hell the whole thing is about.

But it's very disconcerting at first, and I was very, very nervous about making a fool out of myself. Then you look around and see that everyone is working harder than you. You're working really hard, but it just doesn't seem like it's enough. The *Paper Chase* image obviously is an exaggeration, but there's an element of truth in it. You can see how a creative person could take the reality there and stretch it just enough to make great entertainment. And, no doubt, the first year is a tough and unpleasant experience.

In fact, all of my law school years were really years of turmoil for me because, all of a sudden, I felt I was off the track. I had always had this tremendous goal driving me—Harvard Law School. And then I arrived, and I had it, and I wasn't really sure about the next goal. I guess getting a job in a prestigious New York law firm was the next logical thing, but that didn't seem the same as going from Harvard College to Harvard Law School. In part I think that was because of the academic bent in my family; there was just something special about going to institutions of higher learning. Merely getting a salary wasn't of the same order of achievement.

The other thing was that I kind of fell in with a strange group of people at law school. I dubbed them the "rejectionists" because they just thought the whole thing was ridiculous. They questioned everything: "Why are we going to law school? And given that we are in law school, why are we studying things this way?" They influenced me a lot in terms of further loosening the certainty that being here was exactly where I wanted to be at this point in time. And I became more confused about where I was headed, too.

Adding to the turmoil was that, at my father's urging, I applied and was accepted at Harvard Business School after my first year of law school. This would give me a chance to get a joint degree in business and law, but I had no real interest in business. At that point, the only thing I ever read in the *Wall Street Journal* was the editorial page.

But my dad had another student who had gotten a joint degree, and this guy was tremendously successful. My father introduced me to him, and I also thought the guy was very impressive. He sounded like he was doing things that were very exciting: making his own deals, arranging leveraged buyouts. So I thought, Yeah, I really should do this.

Looking back, this was a real turning point for me. It was great when I got accepted. I was thinking, Not two, but *three* degrees from Harvard. Now where am I going to hang that third degree?

That feeling soon wore off. I remember the day my dad and I drove up to move me into the business school. I was really uncomfortable, and it just got worse and worse. I remember sitting through this marketing class on Fieldcrest Blankets and thinking, God, I can't stand this!

I felt like some guy who has played soccer his whole life who now shows up for basketball tryouts. You know that as soon as you touch the ball, everyone else is going to know that you don't know what you're doing. That was my feeling—as soon as I had to speak, everyone was going to know what the hell was going on. And most of these people had been in the business world one, two, five, even ten years.

So I came home for the Jewish holidays and said to my dad, "I'm getting out." We talked about it, and he invited the joint-degree guy over to the house to talk with me again. This time he showed me another side of himself. He said, "Of course you should stay; I don't know why you're upset about the cases—just don't read them. I never read them." He was extremely flip like that, and I couldn't believe he was telling the truth. But I remember that he did sway me a little, and I said, "All right, I'm going to stick it out."

When he left, I went into my backyard to start reading the case for the next day. It was a Sunday, and I was going back that night for class tomorrow. I was reading another one of those marketing cases—this one was about Gant Shirts—and I said to myself, "This is it. I have no interest in this at all. And I have nothing to contribute, either, not one insight about how to market Gant Shirts. Get me the hell out of here!"

So I quit, but not without internal repercussions. I felt what Roberto Duran must have felt after his fight with Sugar Ray Leonard. There's a guy whose whole ethic was, I'll fight anyone, anywhere, any time. Then one day he walked out of the ring in the middle of a fight and said "No more." I sort of did the same thing, and the sudden realization, the shock, that I was capable of walking away, of quitting something that I thought I wanted—it ate away at me. And it contributed further to the sense of I really don't know what I'm doing or why.

It also shook my dad up pretty badly. He thought I was making a big mistake, and I think he was afraid that I might just go the whole nine yards and say, "While I'm at it, I'm leaving law school too." But I couldn't bring myself to do that. It goes back to a concept I learned from Professor Sullivan: what was my alternative? I had no idea what else I would do. So I thought that I might as well finish law school and get the credential. At least I'd have my ticket punched.

During my last two years of law school, though, I was really adrift. I couldn't have been less interested in law. And I approached those years the way a lot of people I know approached college: I did the minimum I could to get by. I didn't even buy books for some of the courses. And this is the same kid for whom getting a B was like getting shot.

My whole certainty about how to approach things had been

undermined by the business school experience. I was afraid that quitting there might have started me down a slippery slope, so I was on guard against that. But the rejectionists were fueling a kind of nihilistic thinking: Why am I wasting time on something that isn't good or interesting? Why am I doing anything? Looking ahead to the future, it seemed darker and darker.

At first, my summer work experience made me feel a little better about going to law school. In each of my two summers I worked for big firms in New York, very prestigious. I got paid what seemed at the time an incredible amount of money. On an annualized basis it was over $60,000, which was more than my dad was making after twenty-plus years. The fact that someone was putting such a high value on my services seemed to indicate that I was doing something right.

On the other hand, during my second summer with one of the top firms, Johnson and Mayfield, my eyes were opened for the very first time. It wasn't like the first summer where they sort of babied you. Now you were given real work; you were evaluated; and you couldn't just get through the summer doing as little as possible. I suddenly realized what it would be like to be there—or at a place like that—after I graduated. That gave me a *tremendous* feeling of depression. I mean real depression. I started thinking, What in God's name am I going to do?

That was when the sleepless nights started. I used to lie there and think about how the end was drawing near, how I was going to spend seventy hours a week at Johnson and Mayfield doing what I knew I didn't want to do. I'd sooner have shaved my head and joined a monastery.

At Johnson and Mayfield I was doing corporate securities law. They have this large underwriting practice, and they represent some of the big investment banks on Wall Street. Every time a client of those banks wants to go public or sell securities to the public, there's a very complex procedure that you have to follow to generate the necessary registration statement. And I was involved in that on a day-to-day basis.

To someone who is introduced to this thing for the first time, it seems like complete madness. I described redoing my law school application thirty times, which at the time seemed like the supreme act of dedication. That was nothing compared to this process. This was like suddenly realizing that although you may be shooting two hundred jump shots a day, there's some kid from Indiana who's shooting two *million*. You're not even in the same universe.

Lawyers, accountants, investment bankers, and representatives of the company selling the securities would sit in one room for hours and discuss a sentence—one sentence. And this would be one sentence on page fifteen of a fifty-five-page document. It was like something out of Kafka. It was hard to believe.

And those company representatives—I thought they were the most boring people in the world. They would talk about the intricacies of the aerosol spray business, or whatever, and I could hardly keep my eyes open.

For my part, I got judged on how I handled a very small piece of the registration statement. For instance, there will always be a section that tells you where you can write to get additional documents about the company. I remember someone coming up to me and saying things like, "Now wait a second here—you've got the zip code wrong. It should be 01741, not 01740." Or, "This punctuation here shouldn't be a semicolon."

I was distraught. I thought, This is *crazy*. I went all these years to college and law school to do this?

In the middle of this summer I came home one night and went down to the YMCA to play basketball. As I was running up and down the court, I started to get into an argument with some younger kid who was enormous—he must have been six-five and two hundred seventy-five pounds. Now I'm not Gandhi by any means, but the probability of me getting into a fight at the Y is about zero percent. When this kid got a little provocative, though, I just turned around and smacked him as hard as I could. And I kept smacking him until a whole group of people pulled us apart.

Afterwards I couldn't believe what I'd done; I'd never had that level of anger before. But I just felt things were coming to a head with the job and with school. I thought I was going to have to leave them both.

I remember coming home that night and telling my father what had happened. It was a very emotional night. But I didn't wind up quitting right then, even though I was tempted. I thought that I'd just better figure something out when I got back to law school. So I went back to the job and just tried to do the best I could for the rest of the summer.

Then when I got back to school, in addition to the sleepless nights, I remember a number of impassioned phone calls with my parents. One reaction I had was to put some of the blame on them, which wasn't really fair. But my attitude was, "Here I am thanks to you guys. I don't enjoy this, and I don't think I'm *ever* going to enjoy it. But you got me into this mess. I'm here because I wanted to please you guys." I didn't say that explicitly, but I had an accusatory attitude toward them. Subconsciously I felt that it was their doing.

Back at Harvard, after that second summer, I didn't really come up with a new game plan; nothing particularly ingenious struck me. I guess it's the same old pattern: just like going from Harvard College to Harvard Law School, I took the path of least resistance. The big, prestigious firms are dying to have you work for them, and they come to campus to woo you. You don't have to persuade them; basically, you don't have to do anything except hand in your resume. So I was going to pick one of these firms, and the only question became, Who's doing something that might be exciting?

At that point I had taken a course called corporate finance. Many of the cases dealt with the growing corporate takeover trend; and it had an outstanding professor and a lot of economic and legal concepts that seemed pretty interesting relative to other areas of law. When I say "interesting," though, that's definitely a relative term. If I had the choice of reading about the Peloponnesian War, Larry Bird's childhood, or corporate takeovers, the takeovers would come in a distant third. But, given that law was going to be my field . . .

Anyway, I looked at a number of firms that got heavily involved in takeovers, and that led me to Curtis and Kraft. I had conflicting emotions about this firm from the start. Even within the standard of New York law firms for working absurd hours, hours most people just can't understand, Curtis and Kraft was considered insane. And that made me sick in the pit of my stomach.

Unfortunately you can't do takeovers without being willing to commit that sort of time. And the more I saw of Maxwell Curtis—he was extremely charismatic—the more I liked him. So because of my interest in the takeover phenomenon and because of Maxwell Curtis, I decided to go there.

I didn't give all that much serious consideration to pursuing something radically different, or even a little different—to hell with radical. I did toy with the idea of possibly pursuing a history degree; in fact, I talked with a Ph.D. in history, now a lawyer, who had written about the German arms manufacturers before World War I. I asked him how he could have given that up in order to do corporate law, of all things. He understood where I was coming from, but he said, "Just as you found things wrong with corporate law, let me tell you something about the history thing. You're not going to sit there and write, 'When did World War I become inevitable?' You're going to write about the production of some small factory in the four-year period of 1893 to 1897. And the money is just a disaster."

So it was pretty late in the game to investigate history or anything else much further, and, besides, enough of the rejectionists' attitude had rubbed off to make me cynical about any alternative. Going with Curtis and Kraft seemed like the best bet.

It's funny. When I did start at Curtis and Kraft, a lot of unhappiness and philosophical concerns I had at law school sort of disappeared. Within the firm, there are little subcultures, and I was put in one very elite group. We were a pretty determined bunch, kind of like the Green Berets. It you have a legal problem, we're going to solve it. If that problem manifests itself at 2:00 A.M. on Christmas Day, call us. We'll come in, we'll get the job done.

That approach can lead to a very unpleasant personal life, but you can derive a certain satisfaction from it. This is more evidence that maybe the people who are less introspective are better off, that it's the Hamlets who are the tragic figures. I don't fully believe that, but I think there's some truth in it.

And I can tell you that Maxwell Curtis made a hell of a positive impression on me. He sure as hell isn't always asking "Why am I doing this?" He's the Larry Bird of the legal profession. His attitude is, "Even though I've already rewritten a brief a thousand times, let's make it a thousand and one. Make it a thousand and eleven. Make it *ten* thousand—make it a *hundred* thousand. . . ." I recognize the tremendous costs and limitations of that kind of personality; but, then again, I can't lose my respect for it—or my wish that I could emulate it a little more.

The main project I got involved in was a billion-dollar takeover battle that turned into a knock-down-drag-out brawl. It was a grueling and often very unpleasant experience. The reality of these things is so different from what the public generally perceives as something kind of romantic. There's endless nights spent eating takeout Chinese food in conference rooms covered with documents; and there's frequently periods of forty-eight hours without going home—or even going to sleep—as you're redoing documents again and again. This made preparing applications for college and law school look like you were filling out matchbook covers.

It's hard to convey to someone who hasn't been there what that environment is all about. For instance, there is a real belief—although some may deny it—that there's really *nothing* that should come before work. That includes marriages, funerals, birthdays, bar mitzvahs, and national cataclysms.

There was one point where I found out about every important episode in the world from the word processing people who were listening to their Sony radios while they were typing something for me at 2:00 A.M. That was when I found out about the capture of the terrorists who killed Klinghoffer. I remember that I had already been up for forty-eight straight hours, and I didn't think I could possibly go on. But hearing that news gave me this surge of adrenaline that got me through the night.

Obviously this was a place where I couldn't get away with being Matthew Goldberg—the kid who kept shooting baskets when his Little League team needed him. My God, Curtis and Kraft is like the civilian version of the Army. And we must have had fifty-five lawyers working on this one project. We had our litigators, our corporate lawyers, our pension lawyers, and our environmental team down in Washington. Everyone was in some kind of unit, and you did what you were told—even when you were told to do the legal equivalent of digging a slit trench for everyone to shit in.

And you didn't reflect very much on what you were doing?

I started to get reflections of a different sort. And now that I think about it, I'm starting to recognize how much of an influence my environment has on me. In the environment I was in, I was with people who didn't really reflect as much as I had in law school. You know that Maxwell Curtis sure as hell doesn't ask himself why he's redoing a brief for the millionth time.

But to the extent that Wall Street lawyers or investment bankers do reflect about things, they are more apt to think, If I'm going to be involved with takeovers and big deals, instead of being Maxwell Curtis I might as well be Boone Pickens or Carl Icahn and go get the company myself. That way I can make two hundred million dollars in the time it takes this firm and seventy-five lawyers to send out a bill for two million. Those were the kinds of reflections I started having.

As a lawyer in this culture, you're often serving very wealthy people; you're helping them achieve something they want. So you say to yourself, "Hey, this guy has nothing on me; there's no reason I can't be doing what he's doing and making what he's making." I thought, There are tremendous rewards in this game if only I can figure out how to use my legal background to get into something like risk arbitrage or investment banking.

In this world of deal-making, I didn't think I was making a particularly clever deal for myself by staying with Curtis and Kraft. To use a simile, I think that trying to achieve material success by becoming a top takeover lawyer is like trying to build the Washington Monument by hand. It's pure physical labor—like running a marathon while you're dragging a piano. And I felt that if I continued to achieve success at Curtis, by the time I were to make partner, there would be three hundred partners senior to me. I just didn't want to be in that sort of environment, to be part of such a vast structure. So that was another reason I wanted to go.

Seeking a "better deal" for himself after several years with Curtis and Kraft, Matthew systematically investigated a number of other Wall Street alternatives before taking a position with a small entrepreneurial law firm in Boston. Nothing materialized with the investment banks, Matthew says, because they sensed that he did not possess the necessary passion for that kind of work. At this point Matthew has worked with his new law firm for the past eight months.

I have mixed feelings about this firm; I don't think it's the end of the search. On the plus side, the money is just as good as it was at Curtis, and the hours are much more sane. I don't work a lot of weekends now, and I can spend more time at home with my wife. I can also enjoy athletic things and even a few intellectual pursuits.

Even though I'm not working exclusively on takeovers any more, which is still the area of law that interests me most, I feel happier with my trade. I deal directly with clients, or negotiate with other lawyers, or arrange to get something done. And I like having people call me up for advice or to discuss transactions. I have far more responsibility now; I'm not just sitting in a room arguing over a sentence.

The big firms want to train you the way they train someone on the assembly line at General Motors. It's the legal analogy of turning the lug wrench over and over again. I'm away from that now and happy where I am for the time being. But I don't really know where I'm headed.

To some degree, I guess I'm still on what others would consider a fast-track path. But I'm no longer willing to subject myself to the extremes of that path in order to win everyone's approval—and to be ahead of every other single person who is doing what I'm doing.

I'm content in the knowledge that there are people at Curtis now who are working on enormous deals while I'm not; who are meeting the Icahns and Pickenses of the world while I'm not, and who are working around the clock—while I'm not.

Every so often, though, the questions and the issues of the rejectionists still creep into my mind. And those are the times I feel a kind of a gnawing dissatisfaction with what I'm doing now. At some point I want to pursue my own destiny and call my own shots; and I get angry with myself for not striking out on my own in some area in law or investments.

But the other thing that is much fainter—and probably a lot more dangerous—is the feeling that, fundamentally, making a good living in either law or business is not that exciting to me. It's *inconceivable* that reading a contract or a registration statement could be as interesting as reading something Professor Sullivan wrote. And I think that something like teaching, even though it would hurt to give up certain aspects of making a good living, would ultimately give me the most satisfaction.

It's still there. That sensitive, intellectual feeling is still there.

A few more things seemed to fit together for me. During the same period that I spoke with Matthew Goldberg, I read this poem by Robert Browning:

> Truth is within us; it takes no rise
> From outward things, what'er you may believe.
> There is an inmost centre in us all,
> Where truth abides in fullness; and around
> Wall upon wall, the gross flesh hems it in,
> This perfect, clear perception—which is truth.
>
> A baffling and perverted carnal mesh
> Binds it, and makes all error: and to know
> Rather consists in opening out a way
> Whence the imprisoned splendor may escape,
> Than in effecting entry for a light
> Supposed to be without.

By now I was convinced that heeding one's inner voice—one's interests and passions—is the only way to find one's "imprisoned splendor" with regard to a career. And, from what I could tell, the blessing and curse of that voice is that it never goes away completely. Even on the fast track, amidst many other powerful voices, it doesn't seem to fade out altogether. As Matthew Goldberg said at the end of our interview, "It's still there. That sensitive, intellectual feeling is still there."

In July, as I looked back on my ride along the fast track, I began to see that I had often listened to voices other than my own. I focused my attention on the outside world and tried to find what others defined as the "right" track to follow. Then I attempted to mold myself to fit the specifications of that environment. In effect, I tried to score baskets in games that I was ill equipped to play. No wonder I didn't become the Larry Bird of anything.

Now, however, after all of the questions I'd asked others and asked myself, I had a different perspective on my career. And some advice I'd once heard from a Harvard Business School professor kept flashing in my mind:

> *Figure out what game you want to play . . .*
> *Design your own rules so that you can win . . .*
> *Then see who else wants to play along.*

Even though I had no money, no apartment, and no furniture, I felt I was finally playing the right game for me. And that feeling grew stronger when Denise Stewart, literary agent, called me and said, "I think your writing is very engaging; I think your book idea is wonderful."

Two points.

But the game didn't end right then. I faced a greater challenge on my next trip down the court. A defender my own size. Tough to shoot over.

QUESTIONS, QUOTATIONS, AND EXERCISES

GENERAL:

    a. What incidents, images, ideas, or words from this chapter stand out for you?

    b. When were you happy, sad, or mad as you read it?

    c. What advice would you like to have given Matthew?

    d. What are the lessons for your life?

FOCUSED:

"I can remember reading passages in those plays [*Hamlet* and *Macbeth*] over and over again just because the pure sound was so beautiful, the way the words went together. The fact that I was receptive to this sort of thing made me recognize that I had a sensitive, intellectual streak. I perceived that this was a rare thing, that this could separate me from other people. So I felt I had to hide that side of me in front of other people."

a. What kinds of things have always seemed to draw your attention and energy, perhaps just for their beauty?
b. To what extent are you hiding or suppressing those passions now? How does that serve you? Or not serve you?
c. How might you give fuller expression to your passions now and in the future? Whom can you enlist for support?

"I remember a number of impassioned phone calls with my parents. One reaction I had was to put some of the blame on them, which wasn't really fair. But my attitude was, 'Here I am thanks to you guys. . . . You got me into this mess. I'm here because I wanted to please you guys.'"

a. In what ways have your parents influenced your educational and career direction? How do you feel about their influence now?
b. What role are your parents (or their voices) playing in your thinking now? Is it appropriate?
c. At this point, what do you need to acknowledge to yourself and perhaps even say to your parents with regard to your relationship?

"To the extent that Wall Street lawyers or investment bankers do reflect about things, they are more apt to think, If I'm going to be involved with takeovers and big deals . . . I might as well be Boone Pickens or Carl Icahn and go get the company myself. . . . Those were the kinds of reflections I started having."

a. What three things characterize the mind-set of people around you? In what ways are you influenced by their thinking?
b. What people do you particularly admire for maintaining their independence of thought and action in your environment? What can you learn from them?
c. What can you do to sustain your own independence and integrity?

"But the other thing that is much fainter—and probably a lot more dangerous—is the feeling that, fundamentally, making a good living in either law or business is not that exciting to me."

a. What faint and dangerous feeling exists inside of you now?
b. Why does it seem so dangerous? What is the real danger?
c. With whom can you share this feeling?

Dodge City Revisited

DENISE STEWART had done her part. After I signed our contract, she sent my proposal for a collection of "high achiever" stories to ten of the largest publishing houses in New York City. But my book did not sell. By early September, I was 0 for 10.

The editors wanted more than a collection of stories: some kind of "narrative pull" or sociological statement. But I went over and over my interviews and could not find a single thread running through all of them, something that I could tie into a provocative thesis or a definitive statement about careers.

Yet at the same time I cast about for some marketing magic, another expedition seemed to be ending. Despite the uncertain future of this book, I could now look directly at others and say, "Yes, I'm a writer—a struggling writer."

With that declaration to the world and to myself, I no longer felt a sense of urgency to question others about their career choices. I had at least a partial answer for myself, and it felt good to admit it. What really complicated matters, however, was my desperate financial situation. Loans can be deferred for only so long; credit card companies will advance only so much money. If my book did not sell quickly, I feared that I would have to get back on the fast track just to take care of my debts. But before that came about, before I had to give up on my book, there was one more interview that I wanted to conduct, one more trail that I had to explore.

I wanted to go back to "Dodge City" and talk with someone in consumer products marketing who had also felt a powerful urge to ride out of town—but didn't. I wanted to hear the tale of someone like Shirley Simpson, another friend of a friend and a brand manager at Procter & Gamble—the badge I wanted to earn when I joined P&G. But I had quit . . .

In retrospect, such a move seems inevitable for me, but it didn't seem so inevitable while I was there. I considered some powerful arguments for staying with P&G. What if I had done so? From Shirley, even though she worked at another company, I hoped to get a better sense of what that might have been like.

Why did I want to do that? I really don't know. But on my late-night flight to meet Shirley, paid for with more borrowed money, I had a feeling that, somehow, my journey of the past year was reaching a natural conclusion. I had started working on this book idea while still in consumer products marketing, and the first person I interviewed was a writer. Now the roles were reversed. I was the struggling writer, and my subject was a consumer products fast tracker.

At times during my trip, however, it seemed as if I would never make it to that interview. Mechanical problems, heavy weather, air traffic—they were all part of my turbulent flight, a flight I would not like to repeat. But when I finally looked out my window and saw the beam of a searchlight piercing through the clouds, I forgot about the delays and the difficulties. I smiled to myself and took a deep breath as my plane began its descent . . . toward a world turned upside down.

The Marketing Manager:
Shirley Simpson

"You don't stay on the track because you like the guts
of your job—you do it because you like power, and
you like to get ahead, and you like people saying,
'God, you're good.'"—Shirley Simpson

*A*S WE SAT ON THE PATIO *eating a huge Sunday dinner, I
began to feel uneasy about the pending interview with Shirley
Simpson. I was anxious to hear her story, but also worn out from
traveling the previous night and afraid that I would not be a good
listener. The large meal, sunshine, and fresh air were not going to help.*

*Then Shirley's husband, Allen, took their three-year-old son inside
so that we could begin. I envisioned that he would return later,
summoned by his embarrassed wife, to find me face down in the gravy
boat; but no such problem arose.*

*Shirley is a natural storyteller. Her voice commanded my atten-
tion, and her energy was more than enough for both of us. My
post-lunch grogginess was swept away by a torrent of colorful and
pointed observations about her schooling, her career, and herself.*

*Many of Shirley's reflections also struck home. I was completely
engrossed from the moment she said, "I had as happy a childhood as
you can have when you're nerdy looking right through the tenth grade.
Tall, skinny, flat, with glasses—you know the type."*

Do I know the type? Heck, I was the male counterpart of that type.

*So I listened with great interest to this fourth child in a military
family who, while growing up, learned how to adapt herself to new*

136

environments all over the world. Since then she has applied that adaptive skill to college and career situations—not always with happy results.

I'm a ham. I have always been extremely comfortable in front of people, and I love the attention. During high school in California I loved theatre and the performing arts—loved it. Public speaking, performing—it was fun, a game. The goal of my life was to be the lead in the senior class musical. I got it and it was just *tremendous.* The singing, the dancing—I felt like a Broadway star.

But that was encouraged by my parents only up to a point. It was clearly a nice hobby, but not at all something that I should do as a vocation. It would waste my brain. And since I carried a straight A average, which was just about the greatest thing in life to me, I felt pressure to establish myself as someone who thinks about the long term, someone who is probably going to become a doctor or a lawyer. So when I said I wanted to go to law school and be an international lawyer, that sounded good to a lot of people, particularly my parents. I figured that out real soon.

At the end of high school I realized that studying theatre might not be such a conflict with law because the courtroom requires dramatic instincts. So I was bound and determined to be a lawyer yet still study drama in college.

There were very few kids in my high school that were geared for college. In California in 1975 there was still a very antiestablishment frame of mind. It was as much leftover-hippie as you can get. I mean these people were so stoned most of the time. I loved them to death, and God, we had more fun that you can *imagine.* But they said things like, "Hey—let it all hang out. Let's get stoned and go to the football game."

My senior year I was totally in love with some guy who was not college-oriented, and that distracted me from really figuring out the best place for me to go. I didn't even realize that there were big differences between colleges. I had heard, though, that there were some snotty, liberal schools up in the Northeast that my father, being a military man, didn't like.

The main criterion for me was to go to a school with a Greek system. That was very important because my mother, my sister, my grandmother, my aunt, everyone—everyone had all been in the same sorority. And for them their sorority life had been the most meaningful thing about their college experiences. So I narrowed it down to the University of Southern California or a school in the South called—let's see—let's call it Touchdown University: TDU. Anyway, they both had the right sorority along with excellent theater programs and courses in international law.

I was accepted at both of those schools, and my parents were going to take me for campus visits so I could make a choice. They were very supportive, not pushing me one way or the other. The problem came the night I graduated from high school. At five in the morning, after we'd been at a party since midnight—we weren't drunk, just really tired—my boyfriend and I both fell asleep while he was driving us home. We ran into a phone pole at a very high speed, and I was lucky to come out of it alive. He spent two weeks in the hospital, while I was in traction for about a month and a half. I couldn't move. I shattered my foot and had severe facial injuries. I recovered fully, but it was pretty awful.

So my summer plans became very simple: I stayed in a hospital getting well and my dad went and looked at colleges for me. It was awful for him because he wanted to be as objective as possible, but he was also a father concerned about his daughter's safety. USC is near a dangerous part of Los Angeles while TDU is in a more pastoral environment. So from his point of view he couldn't help saying that I should go to TDU rather than USC. But I honest-to-God didn't care at that point. Either seemed fine at the time.

So I went to TDU—and let's not mince words here—I absolutely hated it. I went from being the most popular, most loved, most talented, most everything in my last two years of high school to a place that was very upper-class and socially intense like you wouldn't believe. The Greek system and the football season—my God!—everything revolved around those two things.

For example, I wound up taking part of my sophomore year in Spain, which was one of the greatest things I've ever done, but there were so many people who couldn't believe that I would actually *consider* missing the football season and all the big parties.

How could you *survive* if you didn't go to the parties one fall?

And the way the sororities work is really something. They all say that they are looking for people with leadership qualities, but it also matters how much money you have and who your daddy is. And looks count a lot. You have to have the right look for a sorority; you don't want ugly sisters. The pretty, rich ones are in one group, and then you have the not-so-pretty and not-so-rich ones in another. It's real simple. If you don't have pretty girls, you won't have mixers with the great fraternities. And you do want homecoming queens in your sorority, for God's sake.

Things really took a bad turn for me when I got cut by the sorority that all my relatives had been in. It was a scandal to cut a five-point legacy, and to this day I don't know why they did it, but at the time it seemed like the most damaging thing that had happened in my life. The car accident and almost losing my life was nothing compared to getting cut from the right sorority.

It just stinks that eighteen-year-old girls go through these things and that these sorts of values are inherent in the system at a lot of schools. I used to be regretful about my college experience, but now I'm angry. As a senior in high school, I feel I was fairly mature; but then I go to TDU and spend so much of my four years thinking about clothes and cars and money and daddies and getting to the right parties . . . what a waste! I remember getting freaked out sometimes because it was the weekend and I only had two dates instead of three. This is not an exaggeration. I was really focusing on the wrong things. I listen to other people describe their college experiences, and I feel like I was a peabrain, an absolute peabrain. I was so moldable.

It has taken me a long time to get over that. I guess I've always been susceptible to my environment—my husband teases me that I'm a chameleon. And I am. In some ways that's a real strength because I'm comfortable and able to make friends in any situation. Put me in TDU and I'll play by TDU standards; put me in a corporate bureaucracy and I'll play bureaucrat; or put me in California and I'll play that game. I generally do well in any game, but sometimes I spend so much energy in the wrong game . . . then I lose sight of who I am. I'm still learning that.

The big irony at TDU is that the sorority I eventually joined became very important to me in my senior year. I'm still ambivalent about the Greek system, but that experience was important to me.

There were five of us in the sorority who became very close our senior year. We all looked okay and wore the right clothes, but once we took our makeup off, we were very intelligent women. We valued that in each other. And we felt we had something to offer even though nobody else at TDU seemed to feel that way.

The five of us started to create our own currency of ideas, and we started challenging one another's goals. We asked: "What are your ideas and what are you going to do with your life?" Not: "What party are you going to and who are you going with?"

I think we were all very much repelled by the idea of being a typical TDU woman—of going out and just getting a job until you found the right man, got married, worked on your tennis and golf, and then maybe started having babies. I fought against that; I did not want it. I was driven to go out and do something professionally on my own. And my association with those other five nurtured that drive that I think was always there. It had just been stifled and covered up with so much of the crap at college that it had never been able to grow.

It really became a crusade for us to not be mediocre, to rise above mediocrity around us. We even had our own slogan: "Defy Mediocrity!"

All of this seems terribly arrogant now. I look in the alumni book now and see that many people from TDU have gone on to do some interesting things and that they really are a smart group of people. But they had just been sucked into the social environment at college. And there was pressure, real pressure. That's why I think the whole football scandal is just marvelous for the school. If the university will stop putting so much emphasis on football and get rid of all of the social junk that goes with it, it'll be one fine school. No question, the professors are already very good, but most of the students get caught up in the party atmosphere and aren't interested in learning. Studying at TDU was something you did on the sly. You didn't want anyone to know that you weren't being asked out to the right party.

As far as my own academic life, I started as a theatre major, but I couldn't take some of the introductory courses while I was on crutches. I kind of started off on a bad foot, so to speak. I also realized that this was going to be a very different world from being the lead in the senior class play. This was an excellent theatre program, and they were looking for total commitment. But I wanted to get into other things, too—student government, the Greek system, other classes. So I left the theatre program feeling very disappointed that I didn't have enough of the artist in me to match the commitment of these other people. But somehow that was okay. It seemed like there were enough other things to do.

In my junior year, after going through Theatre, Political Science, American Studies, and, finally, Spanish as possible majors, I thought, Bag it, I don't want to major in Spanish. Who's going to hire a Spanish major anyway? So I crashed through some business courses in my last semester and got a major in that.

I still had law on my mind, but I started to think that I'd like to have all my bets covered. And I did enjoy marketing because it dealt with ideas and words. There was one marketing professor who was the toughest and also the finest at TDU. It was definitely love-hate. He was so damn hard—he was just a bastard. But while he was tormenting you, he was still there, still caring about you. I couldn't get enough of his classes; they were so stimulating. And when I got an A from him, it made me prouder than anything I'd done. Otherwise, I kept a 4.0 GPA without really working that hard.

So in my senior year I was thinking about law school or business school, but the last thing I wanted to do was go straight through two or three more years of school. I just wanted to get out. So I looked for a lot of different ways to spend the next year or two—art administration, the foreign service, banking—but I wound up taking a job in retailing with a major department store in Dallas. It was marketing, and it would look respectable on my resume while I sorted things out.

I got what I wanted with this job. The pay wasn't great, but six months out of college I was managing thirty people. Pretty good stuff. Within a short time they promoted me to be the head of women's sportswear at their flagship store, a lot of responsibility for a twenty-three-year-old. That was fabulous, so stimulating. But the hours were horrendous—8:30 to 7:00, six days a week—and the pay was awful: $14,000.

Talk about low-life: some people are stunned at how calculated my next move was. I looked at my GMAT, my GPA, and my extra-curricular activities and figured out which of the top business schools I could get into. Then I compared that to the top law schools I thought I could get into. Then I happened to see an article in *Money* magazine that compared the starting salaries for top business and law school graduates, and I decided that I could do better by going to business school.

So that was my thinking, and I'm embarrassed to say that now. I don't know where this new drive for the buck came from. My family certainly didn't focus on it. I guess I view it as an extension of the report-card mentality: I did like getting 4.0's.

By this time one of my five good friends from the sorority was pursuing a master's degree in English from Harvard, and she got me excited about this whole new world of Northeastern Ivy League schools to which I had never been exposed. Holy smokes! Can you imagine somebody from TDU—total monotony, everybody is the same—going to Boston and a university like Harvard? I mean, it was just too bizarre for me to even fathom how wonderfully rich that experience could be—it couldn't get any better. So when I got into Harvard, that's where I decided to go.

At that time a Spanish professor at TDU who had been a big influence on me didn't think the business world was that great for me. He really wanted me to develop in the arts or languages, and he seemed a little disappointed that I was "selling out." But I remember saying, "Richard, don't worry about it. I think doing this high-powered MBA stuff sounds kind of fun. I'll do that for five years and then I'll jump off and go sell flowers on a street corner in Madrid. You know me, I'm always bouncing off one wall or the other. Give me a break."

Also at the time, I was very involved with a man in Dallas; we were practically engaged. One day I just woke up and thought to myself, If I continue this relationship, I'll never chase my dream of going for an MBA in another city—I'll never do it. So I sat him down at 3:00 one morning and told him it was over. It was pretty dramatic, but I was going to do just what I wanted, damn it, and I wasn't going to let him deter me.

Then, when I literally had my bags packed to go to Harvard, my dad told me that he thought what I was doing was dead wrong. Remember, this is a man who thought of Ivy Leaguers as a bunch of effeminate snobs and intellectuals with their heads in the clouds. And as a Vietnam veteran, he remembered Cambridge as a place where long-haired hippies said that what he was doing was wrong. So you're talking hard-core pain there. Anyway, he told me that going to Harvard and getting an MBA was going to price me out of the job market and price me out of the man market. That blew my mind. I said, "What are you talking about?" He said, "You're not going to find a husband who is smart enough to have the same credentials as you. You're going to be out of reach to the marriage-able type."

It really floored me to have my dad say this—he who had always supported me in my efforts to get good grades, to get leadership roles, and to constantly improve myself. He said, "Why do you want to leave Dallas? You have a great job, a nice little apartment, and everything is fine." The inference was—find a nice man and get married there. He also said, "If you do find somebody, he's going to be some East Coast liberal. How's he going to fit in this family?"

I can laugh at this now, but I was totally devastated at the time. I felt very alone when I started at Harvard because I didn't have my dad's support any more. And I was literally alone in Boston except for my one good friend from the sorority.

So, naturally, I just had a ball—I was just in heaven. The whole thing was a stitch. The other students at Harvard thought I was the weirdest bird in the world coming from TDU. I had hair down past my shoulders and I curled it—and I wore *makeup* for God's sake. These Harvard women didn't know what hit them. They were like, "Holy Cow!"

The face books came out before school started and somehow—don't ask me how—I had a great looking picture in there. Socially at TDU I did okay, but at Harvard—literally there were men waiting to meet me when I got there. I remember being surrounded by men in the library the first week. I was thinking, "What planet did I get off on? Price myself out of the man market . . . my God, these men are intelligent, they're perfect!"

I just couldn't believe it; I had the time of my life. This wasn't what I was looking for at Harvard, but what the hell—who cares? But seriously, I began to think that a relationship would be safe because it wouldn't keep me from reaching my goals.

My third day there, at one of these mixers they have for first-year students, a second-year-guy named Allen—another one who had seen my picture in the face book—introduced himself after most everyone had left. It turned out that he was a Harvard undergrad, a few years older than everyone else, who had pursued a Ph.D. in philosophy and worked for a couple of years with the Peace Corps before business school. After he told me this, I said to him, "My, what a terribly conflicted soul you are." He said, "No, I don't see any conflict whatsoever."

Well, somebody who sees no conflict in that background is either *totally* screwed up or somebody I would really like to know. So we went out that evening and four weeks later we were engaged.

The funniest thing was taking Allen home for the first time to meet my parents, who happened to live in the Washington area then. My father was like, "Great . . . she met somebody. He's much older; he went to an Ivy League school; and he's done all these weird things."

One day as we drove by the Pentagon my father said, "So, Allen, have you ever been to Washington? Have you ever seen the Pentagon?" Allen said, "Yes sir." My dad said, "When was this?" And Allen said, "Well . . . ah . . . I did some lobbying here in the late sixties."

In fact Allen had joined hands with three thousand other people and tried to levitate the Pentagon in 1969. My father's worst fears were realized. But now he thinks that Allen is the perfect match for me.

Needless to say, business school was wonderful personally. I was in love, my courses were great, and I got involved in a lot of activities. It was a very intellectually challenging environment and, even though I was only there for four semesters, I tried like mad to make up for what I didn't have in college. I felt good about my time there.

Right after I finished business school, Allen and I got married. Since he was a year ahead of me, he was already working at a small brokerage firm on Wall Street. I majored in both finance and marketing, the fully hedged position, because I didn't know what I wanted to do. Don't ask me why I ever considered finance, but I did. I have always had a problem defining what I want.

So I interviewed with a lot of companies and had one hundred percent callbacks for second interviews even though my academics were not so great compared to others. My key skill has always been interviewing. I can translate my experience to make me sound like the top of anything—whether or not it's true. But then only about forty or fifty percent of those callbacks resulted in job offers. I thought, Oh my God! Once they scratch too deep they find that I'm just full of baloney. Keeping them fooled was the key.

One of the companies Shirley "fooled" was Procter & Gamble. She liked the idea of getting trained by a top-tier marketing company, and she felt good about the people she met there. Accepting their offer, however, meant that Allen would have to leave his Wall Street job. But he agreed to the move and adjusted quite easily to his new position with an investment firm. Shirley faced the greater struggle.

So we came here five years ago, and Allen has loved his new job from day one. But I hated my first year as a brand assistant passionately. It was absolute misery; the pressure was intolerable. I think I came home half the nights in tears. I'd done pretty well all my life, and I'd gone to a top MBA school; but now, all of a sudden, I was not good enough.

A lot of that feeling came from the corporate culture, I think; it's just so strong. The training that you get starts with the assumption that you're an infant—a blob that needs to be molded. Then they apply the strictest standards to everything. Their niggling process is belittling beyond belief. The pressure presentations, the oral interrogations—I think they prey heavily on your insecurity. Most people are motivated by fear there. For instance, I always had good reviews, but all that stayed with me were the negatives. I thought I was always one step away from being kicked out the door.

They just love people who are approval-seekers, and I'm a lot like that. It was always my dad or somebody else. I've done a lot to get approval. I'm not necessarily proud of that, but at least I recognize that now.

So for the first six months I was miserable and numb. But I didn't ever envision leaving because, my God, what the hell can you do? You're only a brand assistant—you're almost sub-human! And in my situation, I'd just dragged my husband away from Wall Street. Could I just say that we should go back and erase this horrible mistake? Not when I assumed that I was the problem, not the company. And here I was making our marriage and our lives miserable. It was a pretty awful time.

When I started out at P & G, I wanted to become a brand manager before I had a child—it takes an average of four years or so. I wanted the flexibility that comes with having that stripe. But by month six or seven I thought, Forget this. I'm not hinging this decision on my status with the company. And Allen wanted to start a family sooner than I did anyway.

So we decided that as soon as I was promoted or was close to being promoted to the next level, assistant brand manager, we would consider having a child. By month nine or ten, I got wind that I was going to be promoted—which blew my mind because I still thought I was a disaster—and I got pregnant then.

Before I got pregnant, though, I didn't really think about how I was going to get myself out of this mess at work. And what could I do after I got pregnant? You can't interview when you're pregnant —no one will take you. So once I got promoted to ABM and got the pat on the shoulder that said I'm okay, I thought that if I could just get through six months of this, then I could decide what I wanted to do while I was on maternity leave.

So I worked my tail off right up to delivering the baby. I was still not real happy, but it was bearable at that point. Nobody was breathing down my neck saying, "Are you good enough to be promoted?" They knew I was going to be there just a short time before going on maternity leave. That knowledge helped me, too.

When the baby came, I took six months off and did not look

for a job. Then came the most painful situation I've ever faced—whether or not to stay home with our little boy, Gregory. And, if I did decide to work, then I had to find a way to manage my career and family. My parents' values weighed very heavily here. They feel very strongly that if you have a child, you stay home. Period. Over and out. My mother, particularly, was devastated at the thought that I might not stay home.

But I was torn, and I don't know . . . I probably wouldn't have gone back to work if I had felt we could afford for me to just stay home. But we had just bought this new house that we loved based on our two incomes. We had said that if we wanted to cut back to one income, we would sell the damn house and move. That's fine in principle, but when you get down to the execution, it's very difficult to say, "Okay, I'm going to sell my nice house and go somewhere else."

Also, at that point I was very sensitive to the loud signal I was hearing from around the company—that you've got to be a brand manager before you really earn your stripe in the corporate world. More than anything else, though, I was influenced by other women in the company who looked at me as if to say, "Okay, so you've had a child. Can you still make it or are you going to quit?"

Somehow I felt a strong—I guess you could call it an obligation to other women to be an example. And I felt a very strong obligation to myself to prove that I could do it. I wanted to do it, I guess—I wanted to have that stripe. And then I justified it all by thinking, Oh by the way, we do need the money.

I recognized that if I didn't go for it, I would feel like a failure—and feel guilty about disappointing other people and disappointing myself. And I would be doing all of that guilty thinking in a smaller house. What the hell: if I'm going to have a lot of psychoses no matter what, I might as well have them in a decent house.

So even though I thrashed about on this issue tremendously, I finally just threw up my hands and said, "To hell with it, I'm going back to work."

I never, ever thought I'd put my child in day care—that seemed bush-league. But I did a lot of research into different options—day care, live-in help—and we felt most comfortable with a place where some colleagues from work put their children. It wasn't great—no day care arrangement is. But we probably felt as good as we could about the arrangements there.

It took just two months for me to say, "The hell with it; I can't do it." I went to my management and told them that I couldn't do the job on top of my family responsibilities, and I put the blame on myself. Being naive and insecure, I assumed that I was the problem. I wasn't good enough to do it.

The reality is that I had a boss who was driving me crazy. He was telling me, "Now that you have a child you have to be more creative about your work. Get up at two in the morning and work from two to five. In the evening, sure, spend a couple hours with the kid before putting him down at eight. Then open up your briefcase and work for two or three hours at night."

Jokingly, I said to him, "Well, Frank, what about time with my husband?"

He snapped his fingers and said, "Yeah, your husband . . . . Okay, put the baby down at eight, spend forty to forty-five minutes with your husband, and then kind of start slowing down and moving into the dining room. *Then* flip open your briefcase." And he whispered, "But don't tell him."

So when upper management asked me if I was having a problem with my boss, I, being the good soldier, protected him. I said, "No, no, no, it's not him; it's me. I don't want you to lower your departmental standards to accommodate the fact that I have another demand on my life." Then they said, "What do you want to do?" I said, "I don't care. Just get me out of this job."

As it turned out, they valued me, of course, much more than they ever told me, and they moved me away from this guy. They put me on a special project working for a more senior manager. I think they were really trying to help me.

So I spent four months working on this assignment, and I was still pulled very painfully. I wanted to be home with my baby. It is very difficult to leave an infant for a long period; and I wanted to give my family the time I thought they needed.

But I was still operating under that assumption that you *can* have it all—have a career, a child, a wonderful marriage, and keep yourself in good shape—and that you can make more than one emotional commitment. It was simply an executional problem, a matter of being organized. And, right or wrong, the truth of the matter was that I felt very incompetent, and I didn't have the inner strength to say, "This is crazy."

I'm kind of horrified by that now. But having a baby made me feel I was in a very vulnerable position. And shoot, I was working all the time, then coming home trying to spend time with the baby. Allen was *extremely* helpful during this time, and the company kept telling me that I was doing a good job and that they loved me. I also still felt a very strong desire to not quit, to not cop out. I still wanted to get my stripe and do well in a professional environment.

So after four months of this assignment, I was still miserable, but I had reached a kind of equilibrium. At that point, though, the job wasn't very challenging. They had purposely given me a low-demand job, and I recognized that professionally I wasn't going where I needed to go. I still felt that sense of mission. And heck, it's up or out. You've got to stay on the move.

So at that point I said, "Well, guys, how long are we going to do this? We're all here for one reason, which is to move up." They said, "Where do you want to go?" And I mentioned the two toughest assignments in the division. Again, that pull. I didn't really want it, but if I'm in it, I'm going to go for it all.

They gave me the toughest assignment in the division, and as a senior assistant brand manager for two brands, the craziness started again. I had a tremendous amount of pressure—this job was murder, absolute murder. The boss understood that I had to get out at six, but I would come home and work for three hours at night. I was out of control. My marriage suffered significantly; my health started to decline.

So I did this for about four months and thought, This time I've *really* got to get out, and I'm not going to be as stupid as before. By now I was looking at the possibility of getting a staff job where I could coast a little—keep the same salary, work from nine to five. My God, what a coup! So I started to try and create some demand for my services within the staff groups. I had learned that it's much easier to tell your management you want to move if you've already got somebody lined up who wants you. You don't just go in and say, "Get me out!"

Finally, the personnel people called and offered me a staff job in their department. At this point I had an excellent rating, but I'm still working ridiculous hours. I'd work on Saturday; I'd get up in the middle of the night to work; sometimes I'd put the baby down for bed and go back into work. Allen basically wrote me off—it was very tough for our marriage. I wasn't there enough, and when I was there, I was working with our little boy. He wasn't going to get slighted. Then whatever was left of me after that did not go back to him—it went back to my job. My job was the priority. Allen didn't make his a priority because he was picking up the slack for Gregory.

I did nothing but work and see Gregory. I didn't have a spiritual life, either, which I normally have. I had to drop out of our church activities because I was such a wreck.

I'm not proud of it. It was clearly not a job; it was a mission, a crusade, an intoxication—an absolute intoxication. I was totally driven and totally miserable.

It's funny, though—I didn't hate the job. I liked parts of the job. In fact, I liked a lot of the job. But to me, that place is not a job—it's a system, a track. And you don't stay on the track because you like the guts of your job—you do it because you like power, and you like to get ahead, and you like people saying, "God, you're good. And because you're good, we're going to accept you into our more exclusive club and give you more power."

My God, look at the work environment. The trappings aren't so great—there aren't beautiful wood offices—and the pay is just pretty good, not great. So the only thing they really offer is *power*.

Anyway, when I told my boss that personnel offered me a job and that I was planning to take it, he flipped out. He said, "You don't understand. We *love* you. You have an excellent rating, and you're close to getting promoted. No one in their right mind would ever turn down an opportunity to be a brand manager here. Turn off those personnel people because you're in the midst of a disaster if you don't stop this."

I said, "Oh yeah?" But a woman in the company I respected had also told me that if you can become a brand manager, you should do it. Earning that stripe makes you more respected and gives you more credibility both inside and outside the company—whether you eventually move to a staff job or not.

So after someone two levels above my boss also tried to convince me to turn down the personnel job, I realized I had leverage here. I said, "Guys, let me tell you why I'm considering a move to personnel. I want to work with people, to lead them, to help them. I managed thirty people right out of college, and you've given me nothing to manage except account books, a calculator, and a dictaphone. You've got to get me people to manage soon."

Several months later, my boss and I were in Chicago for a meeting. At dinner that night, over a plate of Chinese food, my boss told me that I was being promoted to brand manager for a new product. It was a thrill, an absolute thrill. I was stunned, so totally stunned—but at this point I was starting to catch on as to how ridiculous this was. I was starting to understand the rating system and the fact that for the last year and a half I had been rated in the top five or ten percent of the people, and shoot—I'd been neurotic the whole time. Something wasn't adding up.

So in all honesty, my approach was the same as before—get promoted and get pregnant. My plan was to be a brand manager for one solid day and then walk out the door as fast as possible. Well . . . maybe do the job for nine months and then walk out. I was thinking, "Hey, I've done it. I don't care about proving anything to anybody. I'm not going to beat myself up any more— this is ridiculous. I'm staying home for the next baby, and I don't care if we have to sell the house." We wouldn't have to do that, of course, because Allen's salary had escalated.

So then when I got promoted, it took them three months, damn it, to get me a staff. And I worked all the time because then I started thinking, Can I make it as a brand manager?

I was scared. I thought, "Oh shoot, now the whole thing is going to start all over again. Maybe I'm working so hard because I want to move to the next level." I guess I had established a pattern where I wanted to be at the top and rated the best no matter what environment I was in.

Allen was a little cynical. Well, not a little cynical—a lot cynical.

He *hated* the company, but he was torn because he always tried to be supportive in letting me achieve my career goals. But now he was saying, "You promised things would be different after you became a brand manager."

Slowly but surely, it got different. I got my staffing, and I was the boss. I left at 5:45, and I didn't work at night. And you know what? Having that stripe *does* make it a different world. Maybe it's ninety percent internal, but it was still real for me.

I had thought it wasn't going to be as good as it's cracked up to be. But it is—it's as good as it's cracked up to be. All brand managers say, "You've got to stay; you've got to be a brand manager. It's been so important in my life." I used to think, "The poor suckers. What else are they going to say? They have to say that to confirm to themselves that it was worthwhile."

But it really is some change. The calls from headhunters are significantly better. You are respected inside the company by both staff and line, and particularly by upper management. It's like you've crossed a threshold, and you're not a pup anymore. You are a real live manager.

However, the treadmill doesn't stop even when you become a brand manager. It's still up or out. You can't be a brand manager for the rest of your life just because you like doing it; you've got to push yourself to the director level. And I didn't want to make that push any more. I had my credential, and I had my confidence back. Now I wanted to have a second baby, stay home, and get my family off the treadmill I'd put them on.

So Allen and I waited until I got my staffing before we tried for another baby, and I got pregnant shortly after that. I was still working pretty hard—not out of control, though.

Then I lost the baby.

That really put us in a tailspin. It was not only devastating personally, but I had been depending on that baby to get me out of "Dodge City" once and for all. Now that I had the credentials to do anything I wanted, what I really wanted to do was have another baby and work on our family full-time. So when I lost the second baby, I was lost too. I was in a job I didn't want any more.

So we thought, Fine, there's been an interruption here, but

we'll stay with our plan. We'll have a second child, and I'll leave the company.

The second child hasn't come.

The nice little plan hasn't fallen into place like we thought it would. And that has changed my career perspective more than anything else. I realize that the second child may never come. Once and for all, I've got to get myself where I want to go—and not use a baby or anything else as an excuse.

The last several months have been like Self-Assessment 101. While still doing my job, I've been seeing a career counselor on my own, and I've also whipped out the old *What Color Is Your Parachute?* It's been great, just great. I'm starting to understand myself better and to look at ways I can use my old theatre skills—meeting, greeting, and speaking. I don't know where this is all going to end up, but right now I'm pointing toward personnel or even career counseling—something where people are my topic, my business. And something that's not on the fast track.

I'm starting to admit that I've made huge emotional sacrifices to become a brand manager. Some, I don't know if they will ever pay out. And I've asked so much of Allen and Gregory . . .

Now I'm getting the hell out of Dodge.

As I sat and listened to Shirley Simpson describe her efforts to become a brand manager, I did not feel any regret for having backed down the corporate ladder. I now realized that reaching a certain level— "proving something"—was not going to bring me any kind of lasting satisfaction. The money, the prestige, the pats on the head—those simply would not do it. I would never feel I had proved enough.

Yeah, after talking with Shirley Simpson, I felt glad that I had already gotten the hell out of Dodge.

Or had I?

Looking back, I can see that Dodge City isn't really a place, it's more like a state of mind. And, no question, I carried that mentality with me after I left Procter & Gamble. Finding a publisher and turning my book into a best-seller became analogous to advancing along the fast track; my self-esteem, my self-worth was still tied to the achievement of recognizable, external goals. As a result, when I couldn't sell my proposal for a collection of career stories, my wheels started to slip once again—much as they had ten months earlier.

Back then, however, I had a book, a dream, that provided a new sense of direction. Now I was stripped of everything, even dreams.

Finally, on a Thursday and Friday in late September—in an act of desperation, really—I tried something that Bruce Bunker had recommended, a different kind of prayer. For the first time, I admitted that I didn't know what to do with my book; and I asked only that God fill that void with His will. Nothing else. In a sense, I lifted up my book, opened my hands, and let go.

That weekend, my parents were away; I was alone in the house. I laid out seven stories on the kitchen table as I'd done countless times before. For some reason I stopped worrying about making my book a best-seller—about turning it into some kind of sociological statement. Instead, I began to look at each one of the seven interviews as a distinctly different story; and I saw that there wasn't a single theme that could tie them all together, that could provide the "narrative pull" that editors wanted. I could not point to any one thing and say, "There's the answer . . ."

But I did know that these stories had acted as a kind of mirror for me. By sharing their lives, seven people had helped me to see certain aspects of myself and my own life more clearly.

In a flash I saw a new framework for my book. Why not include my own experience of the past year? Why not lift up and let go of my own story, too?

Right away, the words began to come. Something inside of me broke loose, and huge pieces of my experience from the past year surged to the surface. For that weekend and the next week I did nothing but write and pace and write some more.

I slept little, and ate less. Most of that time is now a blur—except for those hours I relived the experience of walking out on P&G. As I sat over my computer and put some words to the pictures in my mind, images of a desperately unhappy young man, my heart felt as if it were going to break. I thought I was having a heart attack and going to die right then. Unwittingly, through my own choices, I had done violence to myself, to my spirit, and I could barely manage to look at what I had done.

I wanted to get ahead in life according to values that held no meaning for me; and I nearly lost my heart.

QUESTIONS, QUOTATIONS, AND EXERCISES

GENERAL:

a. What incidents, images, ideas, or words from this chapter stand out for you?

b. When were you happy, sad, or mad as you read it?

c. What advice would you like to have given Shirley?

d. What are the lessons for your life?

FOCUSED:

"This job was murder, absolute murder. The boss understood that I had to get out at six, but I would come home and work for three hours at night. I was out of control. My marriage suffered significantly; my health started to decline. . . . I didn't have a spiritual life, either, which I normally have. I had to drop out of our church activities because I was such a wreck."

a. According to your idea of a well-lived life, what elements must be present on a daily basis? Weekly? Monthly? Annually?

b. How are you doing now in those areas? To what extent do you feel out of control now? What are the usual warning signals?

c. What changes are you willing to make? Whose help can you enlist?

"They just love people who are approval-seekers, and I'm a lot like that. It was always my dad or somebody else. . . . I'm not necessarily proud of that, but at least I recognize that now."

a. Looking back, whose approval has been most important to you at different times in your life? What have you done to win it?

b. Whose approval is most important to you now? What do

you think these people really want for or from you? (Ask them.)

   c. What might you do differently if you went ahead as if you already had enough approval to last a lifetime? What do you think would happen?

"The five of us started to create our own currency of ideas, and we started challenging one another's goals. We asked: 'What are your ideas and what are you going to do with your life?' Not: 'What party are you going to and who are you going with?'"

   a. Who are the people in your life now who can stimulate your thinking and support your highest aspirations? What can you do to develop or enhance these relationships?

   b. If you were to establish an "interior council"—an advisory group of six to eight people that you could convene in your imagination whenever you wanted—whom would you put on it?

   c. What is the first issue you would bring to your council? What can you hear them saying? What will you do now in light of their comments?

Epilogue:
Ten Years Later

TEN YEARS HAVE PASSED since I finished writing *Getting Ahead Without Losing Heart*. I now see the way it came to be published as a metaphor for how things have evolved in my professional and personal life; and I want to share this story along with recent updates from six participants.

"I know better now," I think to myself while driving down Georgia 400 from Roswell to Atlanta, where I live and work at Emory University. Ten years ago I had tried and failed to find a publisher to send my work out into the world. Now, having written a book of poetry entitled *Backing Down the Ladder*, I would not make the same mistake again. An hour earlier I had signed a deal with a remarkable woman, Lana Weber, who had dreams of her own—starting a company called Writers Resource Group, which would professionally publish and market select author-funded books. Lana liked my poems and said she believed in my work and me. I chose to trust her not only with my poetry, but also with a significant amount of cash. Yes, I would be going back into debt after having worked not only at Emory, but also in several corporate and consulting roles to pay off my school loans over the last ten years. Now, though, I would not be borrowing for another degree; I would be investing more directly in me.

When I arrived at my apartment in the Alpha Tau Omega (ATO) fraternity house—where I have served as a live-in "house director" for thirty young men over the past three years while working at

Emory's Center for Ethics and leading corporate, community, and church workshops—I discovered I had a voice-mail message from Mary Ann Bowman Beil, a corporate ethicist who lives and works in Savannah, Georgia. At the suggestion of a colleague and friend, I had shared with her a selection of my poems several months earlier. Mary Ann's husband, Deric Beil, runs a distinguished publishing house; and my friend thought that maybe Mary Ann would show my poems to Deric, who in turn might offer some publishing-related advice. As an afterthought I had also dusted off and given her an old manuscript of *Getting Ahead Without Losing Heart*.

Mary Ann's message intrigued me: "I am in town, and it is very important that I meet with you today." Via voice-mail, I arranged to meet her in my office at 4:00 P.M. When she arrived, she sat down and said with a smile: "I have great news; we want to do your book."

"I can't believe it," I told her. "I just signed a deal this morning to self-publish it. If only I had known . . ." And for ten minutes we sat together bemoaning our unfortunate timing, until finally, Mary Ann said: "Too bad. Deric really liked the stories."

Slowly it dawned on me. "You're not referring to my poetry book, are you?"

"Oh no, we don't do poetry. That's what you thought I meant?"

Of course that's what I had thought she meant. After years of publishing rejection, I could not conceive of going from zero published books to two in the course of six hours. But that's what happened. And though I have moments when I cannot believe it still, I am mostly delighted and proud to have two books in circulation and several other projects in development. And through my work with students at Emory as well as adult participants in corporate and community workshops—perhaps even through my writings—I am also proud to have achieved something of the vision I articulated and actually drew with George Dershimer's help eleven years ago: standing on a "platform" of education and experience, doing creative work, and reaching out to others in some way.

What I did not know then was the essential role of community in helping me move toward my vision, find my voice, and live more and more from my heart. I would not have written any poetry, published any books, or become a workshop leader worth anything at all if I did not have a number of people in my life who regularly listen to my dreams, fears, and foibles; who accept me as I am and hold me accountable for becoming more of who I am most deeply, particularly when I lose sight or forget; who also hold me accountable to the larger community and a richer story; and who share something of their own story with me.

I have learned over the last ten years that the only way for me to keep from losing heart is to continually share my heart with others who are willing to open their own. So I no longer think of my life as an individual journey, but more like a shared pilgrimage in which sustenance and direction flow from heart-felt conversations, from hearing and being heard at the deepest level. Success for me now has to do with continually developing my ability to speak and listen as an authentic human being, not with me getting somewhere in particular. Paradoxically, since I have begun to shift my orientation to life—incompletely and sometimes ineptly, to be sure, and only with the support of an ecology of communities—I have received more attention for my work than ever. And I have found myself reciting poetry not only with fraternity guys, strangely enough, but also with senior managers at leading companies who reward me quite well for doing so. I have actually "gotten ahead" in a certain sense by not caring so much about whether I got ahead at all—and caring a great deal more about the conversations I have with myself, others, and life. As those have deepened over the last ten years, I have found myself connecting with new people in new situations in ways I never could have imagined. One conversational thread connects with another and then another—and a path both strange and somehow familiar keeps unfolding in front of me.

Still not knowing where the path will lead much beyond today, I walk and talk and listen alongside others, participating in the weaving, knowing that the threads themselves are not entirely of our own making, grateful for these few moments of sharing with you.

In March 1999, eleven years after I conducted the last of my interviews for *Getting Ahead Without Losing Heart*, and just prior to publication, I sought out the seven people whose stories appear in this book to see if they would like to write something for an epilogue. Able to reach six of the seven, I asked them to consider addressing the following four questions in one or two paragraphs:

a. What is your situation now?
b. How do you feel about your situation now?
c. How do you feel now about your situation at the time of our initial interview?
d. What learning or insights would you like to pass along?

Here are the responses I received.

SCOTT HARRIS

I would prefer that my update just be a declarative sentence along these lines: "Scott Harris works as an insurance agent in Austin, Texas, where he lives with his wife and daughter." To me that's all that is needed, and juxtaposed with my interview, I think it's kind of amusing.

TERRY RYAN

My life, both professionally and personally, has blossomed in the last ten years beyond anything I could have imagined. In fact, I thank God constantly in my prayers for the blessings I have received.

Professionally, my life changed slowly over the course of a few years. Two changes stand out as career-changing events. First, the move I made from New York to Boston. There was no magic in living in Boston versus New York; what changed was my relationship with clients. While I lived in New York, I never really connected on a personal level with my clients. My relationships were strictly business, always confined to phone conversations and brief one-day visits.

Everything came alive when I became an everyday member of the community. Suddenly I began spending ever-increasing hours after work with my clients. As a result, a large portion of my client base became personal friendships. Daily calls quickly became updates on how our personal lives or problems were going. Work began to feel like service instead of work. I started to view my job as an opportunity to help my friends with their daily problems, and it just happens that my friends were also clients.

The second biggest change involved changing firms. Unfortunately many organizations view their employees in a static nature. In other words, once a rookie always a rookie. No matter how much you improve you still feel as though you are seen in the eyes of your bosses as young and inexperienced. When I moved on to a new firm, I was the same person with the same abilities and the exact same client base, but my new employers made me feel special. Interestingly, my clients were responsible for my change to a new company. They promoted my name to companies looking for new people.

The combination of close personal relationships with my client base and the appreciation of the company I worked for resulted in a feeling of complete satisfaction with my everyday work environment. Over the years these trends intensified. God blessed me when I met my wife. She is my soul mate and partner in everything I do. She too grew very close with my clients and their families. We work together, spending time in service of my clients outside of work where the business world becomes more personal.

At this stage of my life I feel a sense of harmony and balance. My job allows me the opportunity to help people and become a positive part of their lives. My wife and I view my job as our partnership. We have integrated my work life with our personal life, and there is a perfect fit.

DARNELL JOHNSON

Our good fortune continued on Wall Street, and I was named a managing director at my firm. Three years prior, however, I had enrolled in evening classes to complete my premedical science requirements. The classes were a wonderful break from the rigors of my work, and I found the study to be most enjoyable. I applied and was accepted to medical school and am now a physician. Soon I will begin training as an eye surgeon. My years on Wall Street were fun and provided me with lasting friendships and the resources to attend medical school. Although each day of school seemed like an eternity, the years flew by, and I am fortunate to have entered a new world. I can't believe how quickly things have changed.

The odyssey through medical school and training never would have been possible without the unwavering support from my dear wife and four wonderful children. Their love provided the strength to carry on.

ALISON KEARNY

I have now been with the commercial bank for twelve years. I am a managing director and responsible for a segment of the bank's private client business. I also have a great marriage, with three beautiful and happy daughters, ages three, six, and eight.

I am so glad I followed my heart and changed course in my career. I left the "in" investment bank to go to the commercial bank, which, ironically, has transformed itself into a successful global investment bank. Then eight years ago, in a move that once again many people thought crazy, I actually left the investment banking side of our firm to go into financial management for individuals, taking me back to my money management roots in college. When I made the move, I felt a familiar sense of awe about what I was giving up, but it has worked out very well.

Looking back on our first meeting, I think I was a bit shaky emotionally. It was tough, having gone to business school, to break from the prestigious track and find my own way. But it was the right thing to do.

And if there's one thing I've learned it is that you have to ignore peer pressure and do what's right for you. I am sure my net worth would be higher if I had stayed at the investment bank, but what is money without a life, without a marriage, without children?

MATTHEW GOLDBERG

Since we conducted the interview, I lost my job at a large brokerage in the 1990 recession and halfheartedly stumbled into another one at a small hedge fund called Cutter Capital. Cutter is no longer small. Propelled in part by the extraordinary bull market of the 90's and partly by its dominant personality, Edward Cutter, it has become one of the largest and most profitable hedge funds on Wall Street. I have grown wealthy and learned to be an investor. I played a significant role in building the firm, bringing in some friends who flourished in their roles, raising money and making many successful (and some very unsuccessful) investments.

In spite of this I feel dissatisfied, even unfulfilled. I do not believe that is because I am temperamentally incapable of enjoying my success. I reached this state through a series of compromises. I chose law school because a predictable and lucrative career awaited rather than the uncertain prospects of being a writer, historian, or pundit. But law was pure drudgery and, besides, if I were going to be practical wouldn't it be preferable to make more money and do more interesting things on Wall Street?

Judged by the criteria I used to make my career choices at the time, my decisions were very good. I have no regrets about leaving law. Had I stayed, I would have the angst without the money, hardly an improvement. In fact a cynic might say that the money allows me to indulge in the angst. Perhaps.

Looking back on my career, I've learned two big things. First, I am convinced of the unpredictability of life and the futility of planning it. When I joined the large brokerage, I thought I had hit the big time. Eighteen months later I was unemployed. And I was ready to leave Cutter Capital after three weeks, convinced that I had made a major mistake. In both cases I badly misread the situation, and I see the brightest investors doing that all the time. Since much of the time I couldn't even recognize the difference between a good and poor decision, I believe one shouldn't get too anxious about career issues.

More importantly, and probably in contradiction to that point, I believe each of us has a destiny and there is no escaping it, only deferring it. Like Jonah running from God's command, I have ignored my calling. But that voice never goes away. Ultimately one has no choice but to understand and obey it. I acknowledge that truth, and I am starting down the path I must travel.

SHIRLEY SIMPSON

I am happily married to Allen and am the mother of three fabulous children aged fifteen, ten, and six. For the last ten years I have been home, parenting my children. During this time I have led a political action committee promoting public education, worked on various fundraising events supporting education, led a family ministry program at our church, and made a lot of terrific women friends.

I have also pursued my interest in helping people think about their lives and career choices and have started to take on clients for career counseling and coaching. As my youngest child will be in school for the full day next year, I am exploring the possibility of doing career development work for a university or business.

I feel very lucky. I have been able to make choices. For years Allen quietly supported my career goals and my job came first. I have been able to return the favor that has allowed Allen to achieve his professional goals. We are able to live comfortably on Allen's income. He is a terrific husband and father.

We have built a loving family. This is not easy work. There is no job more difficult than parenting. And despite all the advances in women's education and career opportunities, mothers are still the ones that do the bulk of parenting and household management.

I have loved the volunteer work I have done. I have worked with doctors, lawyers, teachers, nurses, business leaders, clergy, homemakers—you name it. I have kept my marketing and management skills current through all the organizations and projects I have led. I have loved working on projects that are supporting something I personally believe in.

As I look back on my situation at the time of our initial interview, I feel mixed. I am so glad I did stick with it to get the professional credentials. As I have recently begun interviewing for professional work with a university or business, I am being enthusiastically received. I have been able to take ten years to invest in my family and my inner life. Because of my credentials and paid work experience, I am confident I can shape the next chapter of my professional life to be interesting, challenging, and satisfying.

I believe what I did was risky. I put my job ahead of my family and my emotional and spiritual health. I'm glad I didn't do it too long. But it was an investment in one part of myself.

In terms of personal learning and insights over the last ten years, I have grown comfortable with the many parts of myself. No more self-criticism. So what if I don't know exactly what I want to "be" when I grow up? I am fortunate to have so many interests and skills. I could probably be happy with several career directions. I am getting better at not being a chameleon. I am learning to follow my inner voice and trust my own feelings.

I believe the most important things in life are the old faithfuls: family, friends, good health, a growing relationship with God, and satisfying work. Being fast track or slow track is meaningless. How you behave and treat your fellow human beings is far more important than the track you're on. Power, status, and money do not provide lasting comfort.

Aside from these more personal insights, I also want to comment on three separate but related organizational and societal issues. First, I believe there is a tremendous amount of waste in corporations related to personnel management. Most employees hide their true feelings about career development out of fear. If an employee voices ambivalence about his/her job or expected career path, he/she will be viewed as not committed to the organization. Management does not have the tools and training to truly help employees develop their own career plans. If we did a better job of honestly assessing employees' strengths and goals, I believe turnover costs would decrease and long-term productivity would increase.

Second, we as a society must do a better job at honoring and supporting the work of child rearing. I have observed little progress in organizations providing part-time work options, flexible hours, extended family leaves, etc. And the pressure for women to "do it all" has only increased over the last ten years. I believe children and families suffer. And I know corporations lose talent that they should not lose.

Finally, we need to do a better job teaching young people the life-long skills of self-assessment and career development. We send children to school for years and years, but the most practical and useful knowledge we tuck away in the career placement office the last semester at college or professional school. This does not make sense.

It is no wonder people graduate from college and don't know what they want to do and feel bad about it. We must teach the importance of listening to your inner voice and doing research about ways to develop your skills all along the educational journey.

I believe our churches and temples should take parts of Sunday school time and really help young people explore what God is calling them to do with their skills, talents, and interests. These self-assessment skills are needed all your life as you age and change.

Since I would like to see us make progress on all these areas, I have a lot of work to do.

Appendix:
Books and Films

DURING THE LAST TWELVE years, many books and films have enriched my orientation to life, other people, and myself. Thanks mostly to Bruce Bunker, I now see the authors, artists, publishers, and producers of these works as conversational catalysts regarding certain fundamental questions: What makes for a well-lived life? How can I relate to other people in more life-giving ways? And what makes for a more caring and just society? These authors and artists speak with stories and images that help to keep those fundamental questions alive; and they have nourished and sustained me in important ways.

I think of watching *Chariots of Fire*, for instance, on a dark day in 1987, when I was broke and sorely tempted to go back into consumer-products marketing and forget about finishing this book. I sat on my couch and wept at the end of the film as the music lifts and Harold Abrams walks through the train-station gate arm in arm with his beloved just before the scene shifts to his funeral. He followed his passion and made it, I thought. And I would make it too, I resolved. How would my life have turned if I had not happened upon that movie at that particular moment for a third or fourth viewing? Who knows? I can only say for sure that I feel permanently indebted to the producer, David Puttnam, and to some unknown television scheduling person who offered this nourishment to me that day.

So now in the spirit of a hungry man who tells others where he has found a few good meals, I offer, in no particular order, my lists of favorite books (briefly annotated) and films, informed and limited by my personal passions and prejudices, with the hope that you find something of value for yourself among those you have not already met. Or perhaps you will see some "old friends" to re-visit and explore further. Or maybe you will feel inclined to compile and review your own lists of favorites. In any case, I also include a few practical ideas for making the most of your reading and viewing experience.

BOOKS

Read any or all of these books like a prospector panning for gold. Focus on what the author says about life and what it means to be human and how we can grow in love, health, and vocation. Do not focus so much on how he or she says it. Who cares about that? Go for the gold. Then ask yourself: How does this relate to me right now? What is the "so what" for me? Make a point to discuss your discoveries and resulting questions with fellow prospectors of any age and stage. And keep track of your ongoing conversations with your authors and other friends through journals and notes in book margins; and write in the back of each book those page numbers where you found the treasures to which you will want to return again. Here is my list of some favorite books, in no particular order.

Man's Search for Meaning. Viktor E. Frankl. Simon & Schuster. 1978.
   The compelling insights of a psychiatrist based on his concentration-camp experience.
A Joseph Campbell Companion: Reflections on the Art of Living. Selected and edited by Diane K. Osbon. Harper Collins. 1991.
   A collection of illuminating stories and ideas regarding fundamental concerns of living.
The Sacred Journey. Frederick Buechner. Harper Collins. 1991.
   A memoir that points the way for us to see our own life experiences as sacred.
The Wounded Healer. Henri Nouwen. Image Books. 1979.
   An exploration of how our "wounds" can be a source of healing for others.
The Road Less Traveled. M. Scott Peck. Simon & Schuster. 1978.

A weaving together of helpful ideas on love, personal growth, psychology, and religion.

How to Find the Work You Love. Laurence G. Boldt. Penguin Arcana. 1996.

A particularly clear approach to shaping one's vocation with integrity and passion.

The Soul's Code: In Search of Character and Calling. James Hillman. Random House. 1996.

A provocative way of reimagining the importance of our lives.

The Rag and Bone Shop of the Heart: Poems for Men. Edited by Robert Bly, James Hillman, and Michael Meade. Harper Collins. 1992.

A wonderful anthology of poetry and short essays about mature adulthood.

In Over Our Heads: The Mental Demands of Modern Life. Robert Kegan. Harvard University Press. 1994.

An exploration of why we may feel as if we're drowning (or swimming along quite well).

Common Fire: Lives of Commitment in a Complex World. Laurent A. Parks Daloz, Cheryl H. Keen, James P. Keen, and Sharon Daloz Parks. Beacon Press. 1996.

Lessons and case studies on developing and sustaining a commitment to the common good.

Stages of Faith: The Psychology of Human Development and the Quest for Meaning. James W. Fowler. HarperSanFrancisco. 1981.

Illuminates the "stages" through which our orientation toward life may evolve and grow.

The Liberation of Life: From the Cell to the Community. Charles Birch and John B. Cobb, Jr. Environmental Ethics Books. 1990.

An ecologically inspired model and ethic for living.

The Alchemist. Paulo Coehlo. HarperSanFrancisco. 1994.

An engaging fable about following one's dreams.

Letters to a Young Poet. Rainer Maria Rilke. W. W. Norton & Co. 1934.

Advice and counsel from a great poet to a fledgling one on the art of shaping a life.

Creating Minds: An Anatomy of Creativity Seen Through the Lives of Freud, Einstein, Picasso, Stravinsky, Eliot, Graham, and Gandhi. Howard Gardner. BasicBooks. 1993.
Sheds light on the nature of creativity and seven who have helped define the modern era.

Siddhartha. Hermann Hesse. Bantam. 1971.
The classic story of a young man's search for self-knowledge and a way to live.

The Power of Purpose. Richard J. Leider. Ballantine Books. 1985.
A handbook for clarifying and articulating our own sense of purpose.

Wherever You Go, There You Are. Jon Kabat-Zinn. Hyperion. 1994.
A guide to meditation and to maintaining touch with ourselves and the world around us.

Inner Work: Using Dreams and Active Imagination for Personal Growth. Robert A. Johnson. Harper & Row, San Francisco. 1986.
A guide for working with our dreams and imagination.

The Dream of the Earth. Thomas Berry. Sierra Club Books. 1988.
Provocative reflections on ecology, religion, Western culture, and our place in the world.

In Face of Mystery: A Constructive Theology. Gordon D. Kaufman. Harvard University Press. 1993.
A new construction of "God" given today's nuclear, environmental, and social realities.

The Language of Life: A Festival of Poets. Bill Moyers. Doubleday. 1995.
Thoughtful interviews with thirty contemporary poets.

The Servant as Leader. Robert K. Greenleaf. Paulist Press. 1977.
Practical and inspiring ideas regarding legitimate leadership.

The Heart Aroused: Poetry and the Preservation of Soul in Corporate America. David Whyte. Doubleday. 1994.
A poetic perspective on living authentically inside and outside the corporate world.

Ishmael. Daniel Quinn. Bantam/Turner. 1993.
A dialogue between an ape and a man that redefines what it means to be human.

New and Selected Poems. Mary Oliver. Beacon Press. 1992.
   Read "The Journey" and "Wild Geese" and "Magellan" and
   "Sunrise" one hundred times each.
The Active Life: A Spirituality of Work, Creativity, and Caring.
   Parker J. Palmer. Harper & Row. 1990.
   A spirituality for those of us who do not wish to be monks.
The Courage to Be. Paul Tillich. Yale University Press. 1952.
   Philosophical reflections on anxiety, courage, self-affirmation,
   and meaning.
Men and the Water of Life: Initiation and the Tempering of Men.
   Michael Meade. HarperSanFrancisco. 1993.
   Interpretations of ancient myths with astonishing relevance for
   us and our world.
On Becoming a Real Person. Harry Emerson Fosdick. Harper &
   Brothers. 1943.
   Practical wisdom on what it means to "get yourself together."
The Art of Intimacy. Thomas Patrick Malone and Patrick Thomas
   Malone. Simon & Schuster. 1987.
   Insights on achieving intimacy with ourselves, others, and our
   surroundings.
The Universe Story. Brian Swimme and Thomas Berry. Harper-
   Collins. 1992.
   A provocative narrative of the unfolding universe and our
   emergence within it.
The Ethics of Authenticity. Charles Taylor. Harvard University
   Press. 1991.
   A philosophical discussion of authentic selfhood.
*We've Had a Hundred Years of Psychotherapy and the World's
   Getting Worse*. James Hillman and Michael Ventura. Harper-
   SanFrancisco. 1992.
   A heretical dialogue about the therapeutic model and the state
   of our society and souls.
Synchronicity: The Inner Path of Leadership. Joseph Jaworski and
   Berrett-Koehler. 1996.
   One man's journey and insights related to personal and societal
   transformation.
The Journey to the East. Hermann Hesse. Noonday Press. 1956.

A mystical treatise on leadership through service.

Uncommon Genius. Denise Shekerjian. Penguin. 1990.

An exploration of what fosters creativity in the lives of forty award-winning creators.

Tuesdays With Morrie. Mitch Albom. Doubleday. 1997.

Poignant story of a forty-year-old man learning about life from a dying teacher.

A Year to Live. Stephen Levine. Beacon Press. 1997.

Living this year as if it were your last.

FILMS

I appreciate seeing some kind of life-affirming shift take place for an individual character (or group) in a film. For instance, in *The Verdict* or *Zorba the Greek* or the three Tom Cruise movies listed below, a mostly self-absorbed character winds up at the end with a different orientation toward life. These films provide insight regarding the inner and outer circumstances that retard and facilitate personal development and offer hope that we, too, can develop and grow in positive ways.

Even more, I appreciate films that honestly portray injustice and suffering in the world—and some character or characters who struggle to live from deeply humanistic values in the midst of it all. In addition to Karen Silkwood (Meryl Streep) in *Silkwood,* I think now of the mother (Claudia McNeil) in *A Raisin in the Sun* and the architect (Henry Fonda) in *12 Angry Men* and, of course, the lawyer (Gregory Peck) in *To Kill a Mockingbird.* These characters remind us of work to be done in the world; and they offer instructive and inspiring images of what it means to be fully human even in the worst of times.

So how can you gain the most from watching a movie with serious themes? First of all, I recommend watching these kind of films with other people whenever possible. You gain the benefit of seeing them through their eyes as well as yours. Second, designate someone as the discussion leader. Third, address the questions listed below in the order suggested. For best results: ask only one question at a time; make sure that you stick with the question at hand and do not jump ahead; and be sure to give everybody a chance to respond. The basic idea is to re-create the movie together and in the process discover what the movie has to say that relates to your lives now. So, with a nod to Bruce and Marcie Bunker, with whom I have had the pleasure of watching and discussing numerous films on my list, I offer these questions to enrich your viewing experience.

1. What images or mental pictures do you particularly remember? (Be specific and concrete.) What sounds do you remember? What words or phrases do you remember? When were you particularly happy, sad, or mad? What themes or patterns do you see? What is the movie really about? What does the filmmaker seem to want to say? If you had to re-title this movie, what would you call it?

2. When some kind of positive shift takes place for any character or group, what enables that to happen? What is the effect on that character or those characters? What is the effect on others in the film? What are the lessons for you in your life now?

3. Where is there injustice and suffering in this movie? What brings that about? What, if anything, is done to alleviate those conditions? What positive values are upheld by characters or groups in the midst of it all? What is the effect on others and themselves? What are the lessons for you in your life now?

Here is my list of some favorite films in no particular order.

Silkwood. ABC. 1983.
A Raisin in the Sun. Columbia/Paman-Doris. 1961.
Dead Poets Society. Warner/Touchstone/Silver Screen Partners. 1989.
Zorba the Greek. Twentieth Century Fox/Rockley/Cacoyannis. 1964.
Judgment at Nuremberg. United Artists/Roxlom. 1961.
Schindler's List. Universal and Amblin Entertainment. 1993.
Mother Teresa. Petrie Productions. 1986.
Rain Man. UIP/United Artists/Guber-Peters. 1988.

The Firm. Paramount. 1993.

Chariots of Fire. Twentieth Century Fox/Allied Stars/Enigma. 1981.

Grand Canyon. Twentieth Century Fox. 1991.

Wall Street. Edward R. Pressman/American Entertainment. 1987.

Working Girl. CBS/Fox. 1988.

Regarding Henry. UIP/Paramount. 1991.

Hoosiers. Orion/Hemdale/Carter de Haven. 1986.

Hoop Dreams. Feature/Fine Line/Kartemquin/KCTA-TV. 1994.

The Verdict. Twentieth Century Fox/Zanuck-Brown. 1982.

To Kill a Mockingbird. MCA. 1962.

12 Angry Men. Orion-Nova. 1957.

Unstrung Heroes. Buena Vista/Hollywood. 1995.

Defending Your Life. Warner/Geffen. 1991.

The Miracle Worker. United Artists/Playfilms. 1962.

Howards End. Merchant Ivory/Film Four. 1992.

Groundhog Day. Columbia TriStar/Columbia. 1993.

Philadelphia. TriStar/Clinca Estetico. 1993.

Fried Green Tomatoes at the Whistle Stop Café. Rank/Act III/ Electric Shadow. 1992.

Malcolm X. Warner/Largo/Forty Acres and a Mule. 1992.

Do the Right Thing. UIP/Forty Acres and a Mule. 1989.

The Shawshank Redemption. Rank/Castle Rock. 1994.

Field of Dreams. Guild/Universal/Carolco. 1989.

Jerry Maguire. Columbia TriStar/Gracie. 1996.

Little Big Man. Stockbridge/Hiller/Cinema Center. 1970.

Dances With Wolves. Guild/Tig Productions/Jim Wilson, Kevin Costner. 1990.

Of Mice and Men. UIP/MGM. 1992.

Ironweed. Taft Entertainment/Keith Barish/Home Box Office. 1987.

The Conversation. Paramount/Francis Ford Coppola. 1974.

One Flew Over the Cuckoo's Nest. United Artists/Fantasy Films. 1975.

The Doctor. Buena Vista/Touchstone/Silver Screen Partners. 1991.

The Killing Fields. Goldcrest/Enigma. 1984.

Andrew T. Fleming

FORMER YALE BASKETBALL CAPTAIN, Harvard MBA, and ex-corporate climber at three *Fortune* 500 companies, author and poet Andrew T. Fleming today happily designs and leads workshops in corporate, academic, and community settings on leadership and life-path discernment. His primary corporate client is Synovus Financial Corporation, for whom he facilitates intensive leadership workshops for senior-level managers.

Now a senior fellow at the Center for Ethics at Emory University in Atlanta, Fleming spent five years teaching and mentoring students as the center's program director for Leadership and Life-Work. During this time he also served for three years as a live-in house director at Emory's Alpha Tau Omega fraternity.

His first book of poetry, *Backing Down the Ladder*, is now available from New Visions Press. You can see Andy's web page and send him e-mail at: writersresourcegroup.com